ABC

Reading Eggspress

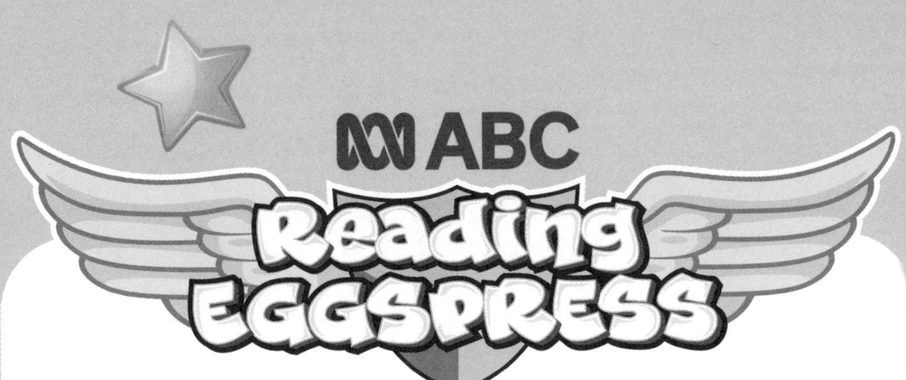

SPELLING

YEAR 2

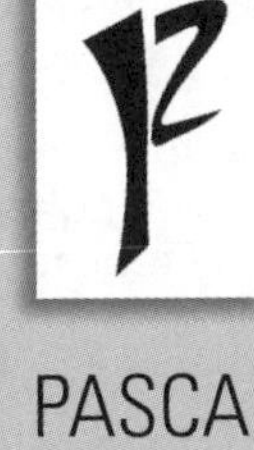

PASCAL PRESS

Reading Eggspress Spelling Workbook – Year 2

Reprinted 2016, 2017, 2020, 2022, 2024, 2026

ISBN: 978-1-74215-307-0

Distrbuted by:
Pascal Press
PO Box 250
Glebe NSW 2037

Ph: (02) 8585 4085
Fax: (02) 8585 4058

Email: info@blake.com.au
Website: www.blake.com.au

Publisher: Katy Pike
Series editor: Amy Russo
Editors: Laura Anderson, Stacey Belgre
Designed and typeset by The Modern Art Production Group
Printed in China by 1010 Printing International Ltd

CONTENTS

WHAT IS READING EGGSPRESS?

Reading Eggspress is an online program designed to build language and literacy skills for students in Years 1 – 6. The program has targeted lesson sequences for Comprehension, Spelling, Grammar and Punctuation that align with national curriculum standards for achievement. With built-in rewards, access to over 4000 e-books and rich assessment data to track progress, the Reading Eggspress program individualises learning to help students achieve their personal best.

How does the Reading Eggspress Spelling Program work?

Research proves that students have more spelling success if they learn to recognise common spelling patterns and generalisations as part of an explicit and systematic teaching program. The *Reading Eggspress Spelling program* focuses on common spelling rules, generalisations and strategies using a combination of teaching videos, engaging online activities, games and tests with fully integrated student books.

The *Reading Eggspress Spelling books* for Years 1 – 6 extend students as they learn, use and apply their spelling skills across a range of written activities. The student books work alongside the online program to reinforce learning for each lesson.

The *Reading Eggspress Spelling program* is structured to provide instruction on a spelling rule, strategy or generalisation with 36 lessons per year level. Each lesson is centred on a carefully crafted word list, based around the sound, structure or meaning features of words. These word lists have been created by consulting educational research and the Australian Curriculum.

Self-paced systematic program

Easy to understand videos

Assessment and instant feedback

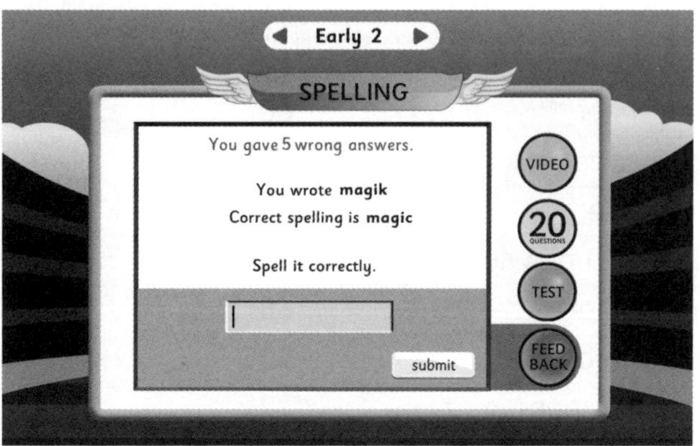

Practice activities

Reading Eggspress Spelling and the Australian Curriculum

Each lesson focuses on a core set of 20 words and 10 challenge words to extend students. These lists have been created to align with the Australian Curriculum Content Descriptions and Elaborations.

Year 2 Language

Expressing and developing ideas

ACELA1471

Understand how to use digraphs, long vowels, blends and silent letters to spell words, and use morphemes and syllabification to break up simple words and use visual memory to write irregular words

- drawing on knowledge of high frequency sight words
- drawing on knowledge of sound–letter relationships (for example breaking words into syllables and phonemes)
- using known words in writing and spell unknown words using developing visual, graphophonic and morphemic knowledge

ACELA1472

Recognise common prefixes and suffixes and how they change a word's meaning

- joining discussion about how a prefix or suffix affects meaning, for example 'uncomfortable', 'older', and 'division'

Sound and letter knowledge

ACELA1474

Recognise most sound–letter matches including silent letters, vowel/consonant digraphs and many less common sound–letter combinations

- recognising when some letters are silent, for example 'knife', 'listen', 'castle', and providing the sound for less common sound–letter matches, for example 'tion'

Reading Eggspress Spelling

Each lesson uses a combination of activities from the following categories:

Proofreading: self-directed checking of written text. Proofreading assists the development of reading and writing.

Visual memory: the Look-say-cover-write-check creates a visual memory of the word. It is important as a self-correction skill.

Definitions: morphemic understanding of words. This skill is used selectively where an understanding of the etymology and morphological structure benefits orthographic understanding.

Word families: groups of words that share common morphemes. Identifying visual and morphemic commonalities aids accurate spelling and is used throughout the program.

Word sorts: groups of words that share a common theme. Word sorts have been integrated as grouping together like ideas helps learners make sense of the world around them.

Overview of Spelling Aspects Covered in Year 2

Spelling Aspect	Areas Covered	Pages
Digraphs and trigraphs	ar, or; scr, spr, str; qu; wh; kn, gn, wr; a-e, e-e, i-e, o-e, u-e; ea, ee; ai, a-e	4, 5, 8, 9, 10, 11, 26, 27, 36, 37, 58, 59, 60, 61, 64, 65
Endings	y, ey; le, el, al; ge; ar, er, or	6, 7, 20, 21, 24, 25, 48, 49, 62, 63
Prefixes	un	14, 15
Suffixes	ing, ed; s, ies; s, es; ful, less; er, est; ly; ment, ness	12, 13, 30, 31, 34, 35, 38, 39, 42, 43, 46, 47, 54, 55, 68, 69, 72, 73
Letter patterns	k, ck	44, 45
Other aspects of spelling	verb endings; vowel sounds; soft c; j sound; exceptions; oo sound; homophones; compound words; irregular verbs; word building; tricky words	2, 3, 16, 17, 18, 19, 22, 23, 28, 29, 32, 33, 40, 41, 50, 51, 56, 57, 66, 67, 70, 71

MY PROGRESS CHART • LESSONS 2.1 – 2.18

Name ______________________________

Lesson	Level	Online test score	Pages	Self-assessment *With this list I feel ...*
2.1 Verb endings: s, es		/10	2 - 3	
2.2 ar and or		/10	4 - 5	
2.3 y and ey		/10	6 - 7	
2.4 scr, spr, str		/10	8 - 9	
2.5 qu		/10	10 - 11	
2.6 ing, ed		/10	12 - 13	
2.7 Prefix: un		/10	14 - 15	
2.8 oo		/10	16 - 17	
2.9 Soft c		/10	18 - 19	
2.10 Plurals with y		/10	20 - 21	
2.11 j sound		/10	22 - 23	
2.12 Endings: le, el, al		/10	24 - 25	
2.13 wh		/10	26 - 27	
2.14 Exceptions		/10	28 - 29	
2.15 Plurals		/10	30 - 31	
2.16 oo sound		/10	32 - 33	
2.17 Suffixes: ful, less		/10	34 - 35	
2.18 kn, gn, wr		/10	36 - 37	

MY PROGRESS CHART • LESSONS 2.19 – 2.36

Name ______________________________

Lesson	Level	Online test score	Pages	Self-assessment *With this list I feel ...*
2.19 er, est		/10	38 - 39	
2.20 Homophones		/10	40 - 41	
2.21 ing, ed		/10	42 - 43	
2.22 k sound		/10	44 - 45	
2.23 Suffix: ly		/10	46 - 47	
2.24 Ending: ge		/10	48 - 49	
2.25 Compound words		/10	50 - 51	
2.26 Contractions		/10	52 - 53	
2.27 Plurals		/10	54 - 55	
2.28 Past tense		/10	56 - 57	
2.29 a-e, e-e, i-e, o-e, u-e		/10	58 - 59	
2.30 ea and ee		/10	60 - 61	
2.31 Endings: ar, er, or		/10	62 - 63	
2.32 ai, a-e		/10	64 - 65	
2.33 Word building		/10	66 - 67	
2.34 er, est		/10	68 - 69	
2.35 Tricky words		/10	70 - 71	
2.36 ment, ness		/10	72 - 73	

Suffixes – adding s and es

1 Copy each list word.

chops ______	melts ______	dances ______
bites ______	hammers ______	listens ______
bumps ______	crosses ______	blesses ______
fixes ______	breaks ______	munches ______
grows ______	buys ______	pushes ______
chases ______	behaves ______	coaches ______
hurts ______	covers ______	

2 Correct it. Write the word correctly.

She dancess to the music. ______

He lissens to the music. ______

Mario breeks the stick in half. ______

Dad buyes food at the shops. ______

Leila puushes her brother on the swing. ______

3 Unscramble it. Unscramble the letters to make a list word.

ssescro ______	versco ______
ltsme ______	havesbe ______
chescoa ______	ersmham ______

4 Name it. Write the name for each.

m ______

d ______

b ______

Suffixes – adding s and es

5 Turn each word into a list word.

chop	chops
break	
push	
grow	
bite	

Challenge words

6 Copy each challenge word.

polishes ____________ finishes ____________
vanishes ____________ switches ____________
touches ____________ attaches ____________
launches ____________ measures ____________
teaches ____________ guesses ____________

7 Silly sentences. Use as many challenge words as possible to make a silly story.

____
____
____

8 Choose it. Circle the correct word to complete the sentence.

Dad always [finishes] [feneshes] his dinner before me.
The carpenter [measores] [measures] each piece of wood.
The rain [vanishes] [vaneshes] when the sun comes out.
Jack [teeches] [teaches] his dog how to fetch.
Before going to bed, Dad [switches] [swetches] off all the lights.

Vowel digraphs – ar, or

2.2

1 Copy each list word.

arm	ward	wart
war	warn	warp
car	born	apart
worm	storm	sport
work	short	spark
warm	shark	stork
word	snort	

2 Label it. Label the pictures using list words.

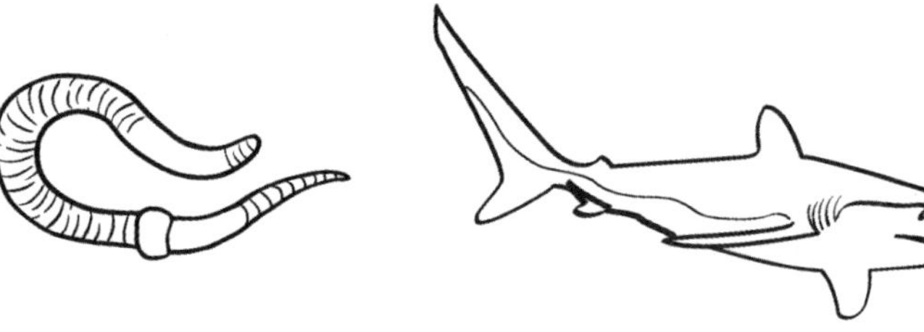

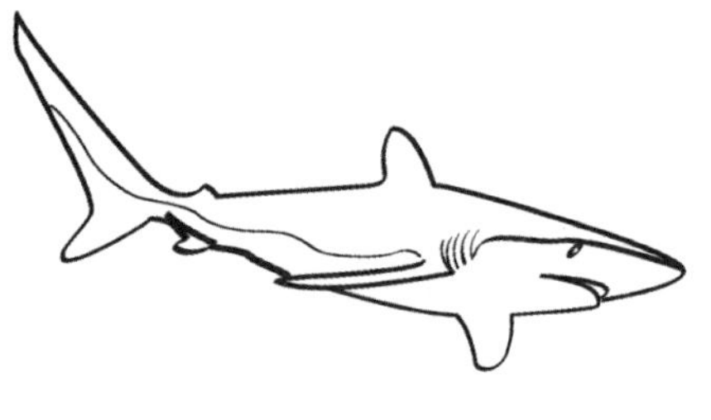

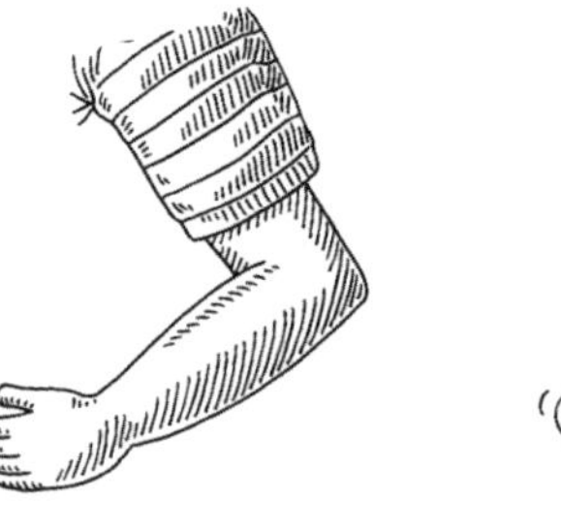

w ____ s ____ a ____ s ____

3 Sort it.

ar

or

Vowel digraphs – ar, or

4 Missing word. Fill in the missing word.

In summer the weather is very __________.

Cricket is my favourite __________.

Mum drove us to school in her new __________.

A __________ has a large fin and lives in the ocean.

The goblin had a huge __________ on his nose.

Challenge words

5 Copy each challenge word.

morning	__________	worth	__________
corner	__________	wharf	__________
normal	__________	towards	__________
world	__________	worship	__________
worse	__________	remark	__________

6 Words within words. Make six words using letters from **towards**.

__________ __________ __________

__________ __________ __________

7 Choose it. Circle and rewrite the correct word to complete the sentence.

I have breakfast in the [morning] [moorning]. __________

We saw boats tied up to the [wherf] [wharf]. __________

We bought ice-cream at the [corner] [cerner] shop. __________

They ran [towards] [toowards] the finish line. __________

Word endings – y, ey

1 Copy each list word.

any	______	worry	______	empty	______
many	______	sixty	______	trolley	______
ugly	______	honey	______	ninety	______
key	______	busy	______	hockey	______
money	______	twenty	______	seventy	______
donkey	______	turkey	______	pretty	______
valley	______	fairy	______		

2 Unscramble it. Unscramble the letters to make a list word.

ckhoey	______	onmey	______
nenity	______	typret	______
neyho	______	rutkey	______

3 Name it. Write the name for each.

t ______

m ______

t ______

k ______

4 Correct it. Write the word that is wrong correctly.

She put her muney in her purse. ______

My grandma is ninty years old. ______

I pushed the troley through the supermarket. ______

I spread a lot of huney onto my toast. ______

Word endings – y, ey

5 Alphabet. Put these list words into alphabetical order.

fairy any ugly donkey empty

__________ __________ __________ __________ __________

Challenge words

6 Copy each challenge word.

parsley	__________	library	__________
family	__________	chimney	__________
country	__________	every	__________
jersey	__________	January	__________
journey	__________	February	__________

7 Interesting question. Answer the question with a challenge word.

What does smoke come out of? __________

What is the first month of the year? __________

Where can you find lots of books? __________

What grows in a herb garden? __________

Who do you live with? __________

8 Solve it. Read the clue and complete the sentence.

I am a shirt you wear while playing sport. I am a __________.

I come right after January. I am __________.

I allow you to read and borrow books. I am a __________.

I am the land outside big cities. I am the __________.

Words that start with – scr, spr and str

1 Copy each list word.

street	______	sprint	______	stream	______
spray	______	scrape	______	string	______
scrub	______	strip	______	scream	______
strong	______	strain	______	streak	______
stroke	______	struck	______	stride	______
strap	______	stripe	______	spring	______
strike	______	screen	______		

2 Sort it.

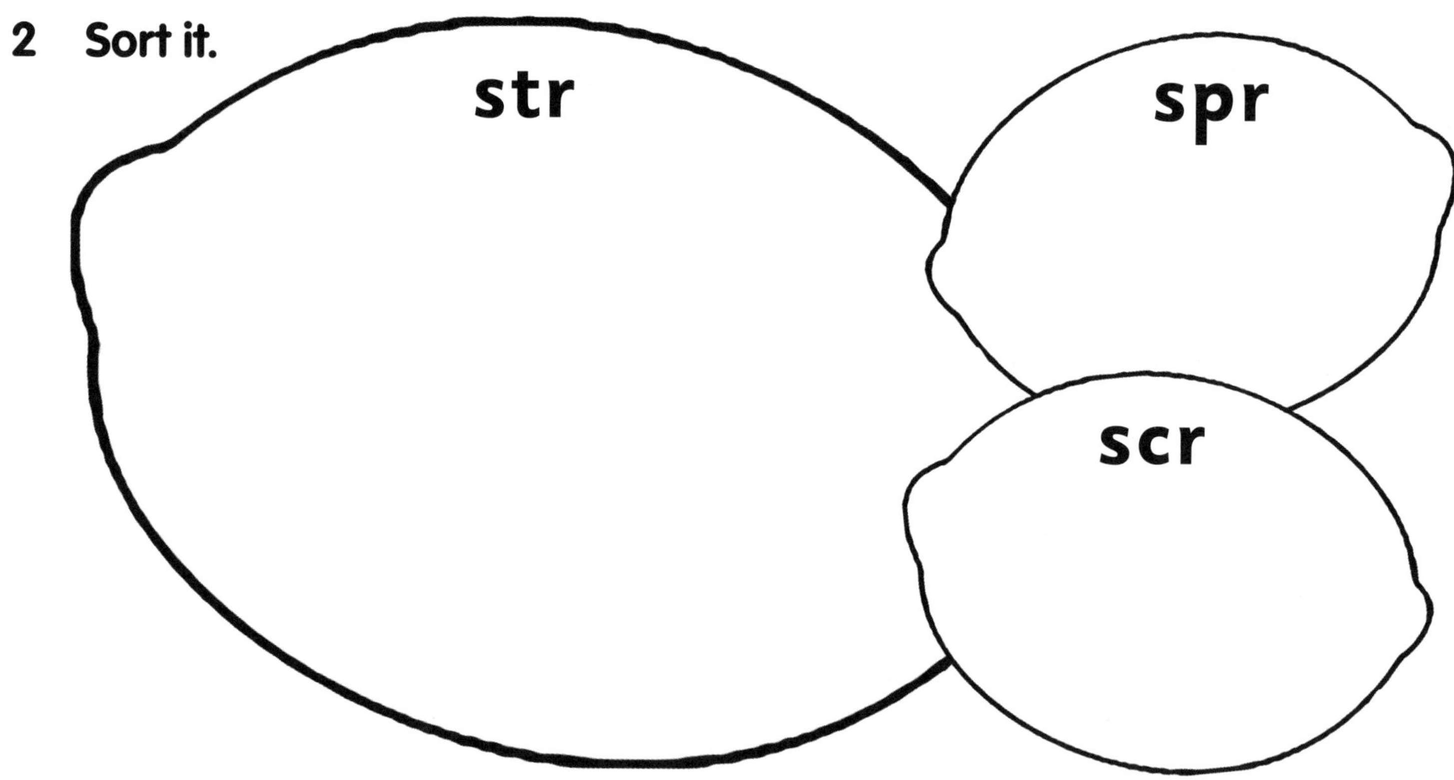

3 Word shapes. Match these list words to their word shapes.

stroke **street** **strap** **strain** **scrub**

Words that start with – scr, spr and str

4 Correct it. Write the word that is wrong correctly.

The kitten played with the ball of streng. __________

Cody tripped over at the start of the sprent. __________

My sister was blocking the television scren. __________

Our dog has a white strype on his head. __________

On hot days we swim in the cool streem. __________

Challenge words

5 Copy each challenge word.

strange	__________	strength	__________
stroll	__________	struggle	__________
scribble	__________	screech	__________
scramble	__________	strict	__________
sprinkle	__________	sprout	__________

6 Choose it. Circle and rewrite the correct word to complete the sentence.

Grandma is very [strect] [strict]. __________

We took a [stroll] [strolle] along the beach. __________

I saw the car [screech] [screach] to a stop. __________

I used my umbrella when it started
to [sprinkle] [sprenkle] with rain. __________

7 Silly sentences. Use as many challenge words as possible to make a silly story.

____

____

____

Digraph – qu

1 Copy each list word.

queen	______	quill	______	quake	______
quiz	______	quilt	______	squint	______
quack	______	quote	______	query	______
quit	______	equal	______	quiver	______
quite	______	equip	______	squeak	______
quest	______	quail	______	squirrel	______
quiet	______	quaint	______		

2 Rhyming words.

shake, make, ______ scene, bean, ______

shiver, liver, ______ wrote, float, ______

chest, best, ______ whizz, fizz, ______

3 Riddles. Which list word answers the riddle?

I live in a castle and sit on a throne. ______

A mouse makes this sound. ______

I like acorns and have a big furry tail. ______

You put me on your bed when it gets cold. ______

A duck makes this sound. ______

4 Name it. Write the name for each.

q ______

q ______

s ______

Digraph – qu

5 Missing letters. Write the missing letters.

__ qua __   __ __ it   eq __ i __

q __ es __   qu __ t __   qu __ i __ t

Challenge words

6 Copy each challenge word.

queasy	________	sequin	________
squelch	________	require	________
qualify	________	quench	________
quarrel	________	question	________
frequent	________	squabble	________

7 Choose it. Circle and rewrite the correct word to complete the sentence.

I felt [queasy] [qweasy] after eating too many lollies. ________

I drank water to [qwench] [quench] my thirst. ________

I raised my hand to ask her a [question] [qwestion]. ________

I heard the snail [sqwelch] [squelch] under my shoe. ________

8 Chunks. Rearrange the chunks to make a list word.

qu fre ent ________

ab squ ble ________

es on ti qu ________

en ch qu ________

el ch squ ________

ire re qu ________

Suffixes – ing, ed

1 Copy each list word.

saving ______	chased ______	teased ______
closed ______	agreed ______	shaped ______
hiking ______	giving ______	writing ______
freed ______	sharing ______	gazing ______
posing ______	changed ______	solved ______
used ______	phoned ______	exploded ______
raced ______	wasting ______	

2 Sort it.

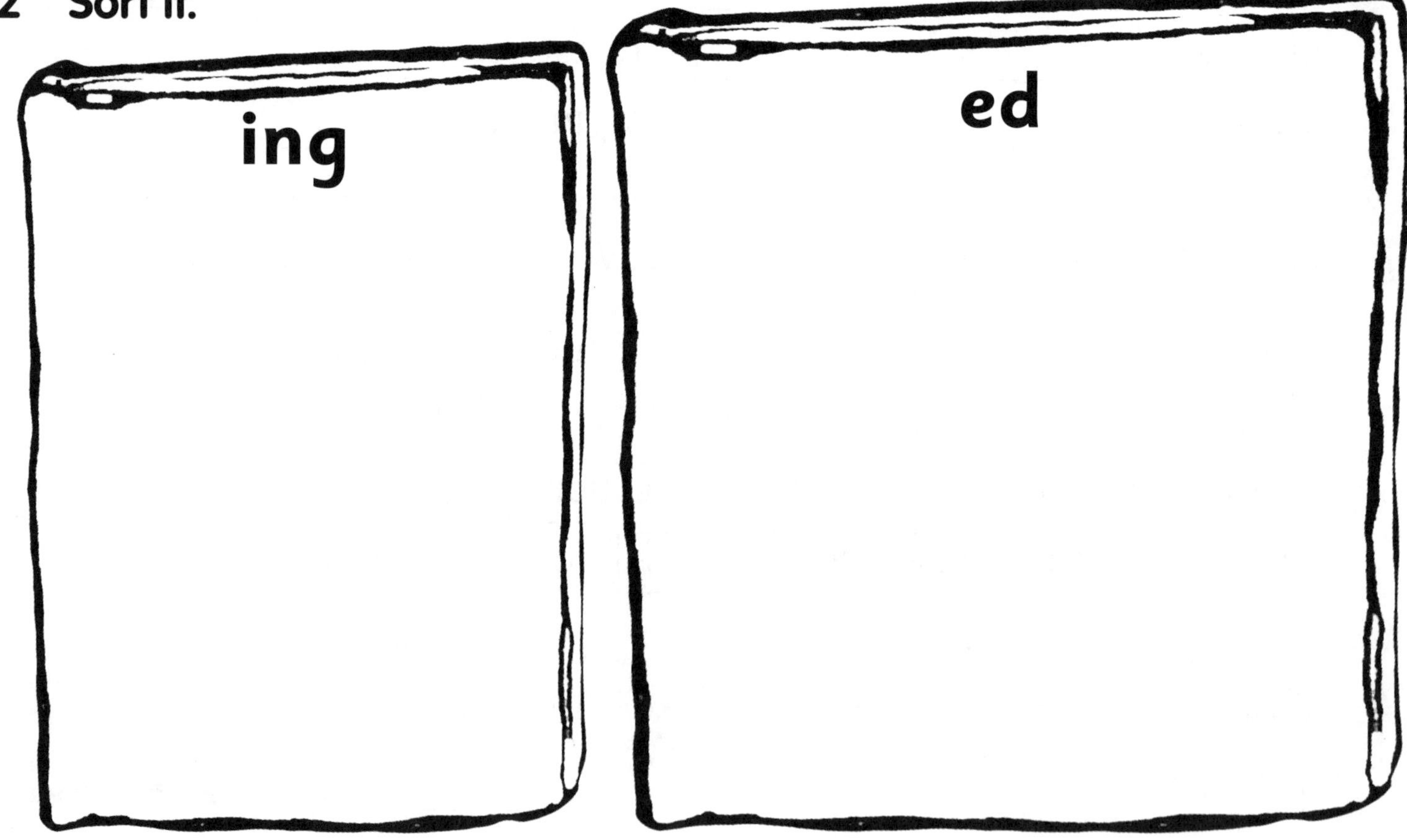

3 Unscramble it. Unscramble the letters to make a list word.

sedclo ______	hsaring ______
kihing ______	singpo ______
angedch ______	eedfr ______

Suffixes – ing, ed

4 Correct it. Write the word that is wrong correctly.

The dog chaased the cat around the garden. ______

The balloon explooded during the party. ______

He finally sollved the puzzle. ______

I agred to help set up the cake stall. ______

Challenge words

5 Copy each challenge word.

arriving ______ created ______

argued ______ freezing ______

chuckling ______ survived ______

caused ______ completed ______

shining ______ compared ______

6 Choose it. Circle and rewrite the correct word to complete the sentence.

The weather was [freezing] [frezing] outside. ______

My brother and I [creeated] [created] a secret code. ______

We will be [ariving] [arriving] late because of traffic. ______

You will get a medal when you have [completed] [coompleted] the race. ______

7 Silly sentences. Use as many challenge words as possible to make a silly story.

______

______

______

Prefix – un

1 Copy each list word.

undo ______	unmade ______	unhappy ______
undid ______	unfair ______	undone ______
untie ______	unlike ______	unroll ______
unwise ______	unstuck ______	unable ______
unsafe ______	untrue ______	unwind ______
unfit ______	untidy ______	unload ______
unkind ______	unlock ______	

2 Opposites.

stuck	unstuck	happy	______
roll	______	able	______
kind	______	made	______
wind	______	true	______

3 Missing letters. Write the missing letters.

_ _ fai _	_ nlik _	_ _ wis _
_ _ load	u _ sa _ e	_ _ fi _

4 Addition words.

un	+	true	=	
un	+	fold	=	
un	+	happy	=	

Prefix – un

Challenge words

5 Copy each challenge word.

unlucky	__________	unwrap	__________
unknown	__________	uneven	__________
unbuckle	__________	unhelpful	__________
unusual	__________	unhealthy	__________
untangle	__________	unfriendly	__________

6 Words within words. Make six words using the letters in **unfriendly**.

__________ __________ __________

__________ __________ __________

7 Choose it. Circle and rewrite the correct word to complete the sentence.

Some people think that black cats are [unlucky] [unluky]. __________

I will [unwrappe] [unwrap] my birthday presents. __________

The [unfriendly] [unfrendly] dog barks all the time. __________

I helped my sister [unbuckel] [unbuckle] her seatbelt. __________

8 Hidden words. Find the challenge word.

djfunhealthysfdf __________

dfdunhelpfuldfsdfv __________

dfdfunusualdfdfs __________

dfdduntangledfd __________

Vowel sounds – short and long oo

1 Copy each list word.

too ______	hoot ______	goose ______
mood ______	took ______	proof ______
hook ______	cool ______	shoot ______
foot ______	tooth ______	loose ______
wood ______	broom ______	groom ______
room ______	gloom ______	ooze ______
soon ______	igloo ______	

2 Name it. Write the name for each.

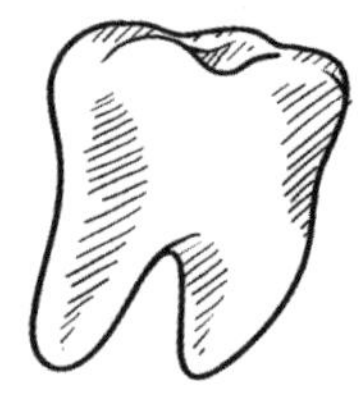

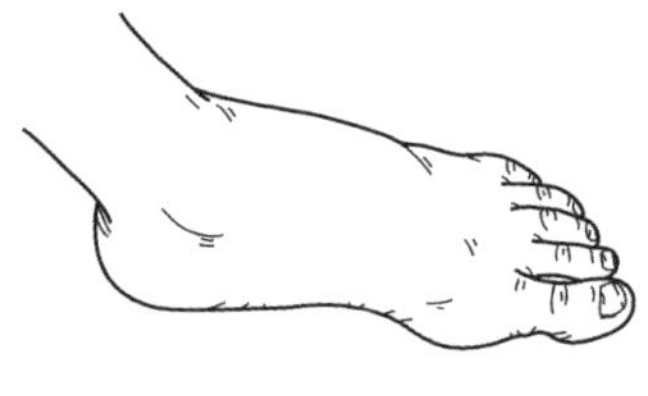

t 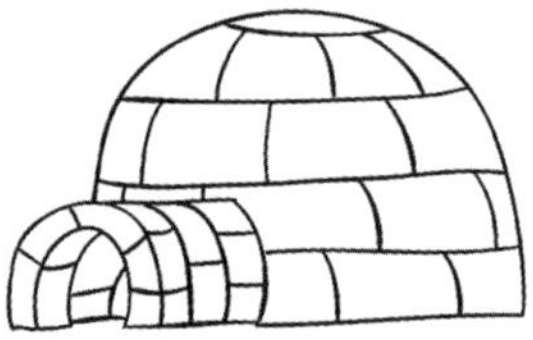 ______ i ______ f ______ h ______

3 Sort the sounds.

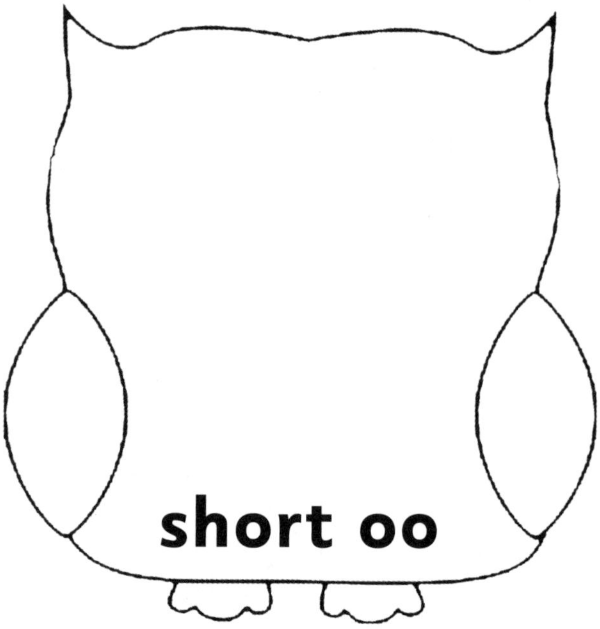

short oo

long oo

Vowel sounds – short and long oo

4 Fill in the missing letters.

Mum told me to clean my r__________.

I swept up the mess with a b__________.

He cut blocks of ice to build an i__________.

Challenge words

5 Copy each challenge word.

soothe	____________	poodle	____________
scooter	____________	boomerang	____________
rooster	____________	kangaroo	____________
school	____________	snooze	____________
goodbye	____________	cocoon	____________

6 Solve it. Read the clue and complete the sentence.

I live on a farm and sing very loudly. I am a ____________.

If you throw me, I will come back. I am a ____________.

I have two wheels and a handle bar. I am a ____________.

I am a dog with thick curly fur. I am a ____________.

A caterpillar goes in, a butterfly comes out. I am a ____________.

7 Interesting question. Answer the question with a challenge word.

What do you say when you are leaving? ____________

Where do you go during the week? ____________

What has a pouch and two large feet? ____________

Soft c

1 Copy each list word.

race	______	trace	______	since	______
ice	______	once	______	price	______
cell	______	slice	______	space	______
city	______	twice	______	grace	______
mice	______	cycle	______	spicy	______
face	______				
icy	______				
lace	______				
nice	______				
pace	______				

2 Name it. Write the name for each.

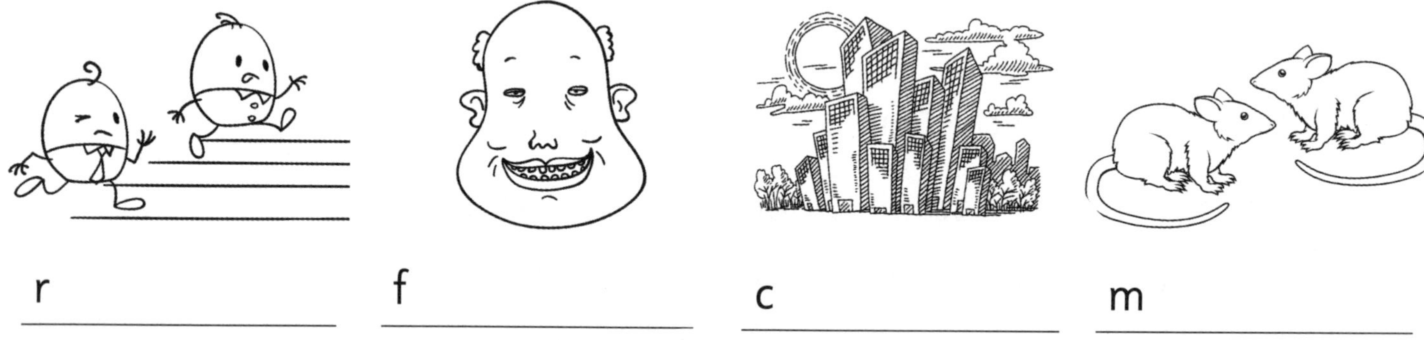

r ______ f ______ c ______ m ______

3 Fill in the missing letters.

Her dress was fringed with white l__ __e.

On my birthday I was given the biggest s__ __ __e of cake.

I enjoyed the movie so much I saw it t__ __ __e.

My drink was i__ __-cold.

O__ __e upon a time there was a beautiful princess.

It was n__ __e of him to stay and help us clean up.

Soft c

4 Word shapes. Match these list words to their word shapes.

cell spicy space race city

Challenge words

5 Copy each challenge word.

fleece	______	prince	______
peace	______	recite	______
juicy	______	pencil	______
fancy	______	notice	______
piece	______	excite	______

6 Choose it. Circle the correct word to complete the sentence.

The peach was so [juicy] [joocy] it squirted all over me.

I used a yellow [pencel] [pencil] to colour in the sun.

The [prynce] [prince] was searching for the princess.

My boots have a soft [flece] [fleece] lining.

I just wanted one more [pece] [piece] of chocolate.

7 Interesting question. Answer the question with a challenge word.

What comes from a sheep? ______

What do you write with? ______

Who is the king's son? ______

Suffixes – adding es to words ending in y 2.10

1 Copy each list word.

cries	______	babies	______	ladies	______
dries	______	stories	______	entries	______
fries	______	parties	______	worries	______
spies	______	carries	______	replies	______
skies	______	cities	______	studies	______
tries	______	bodies	______	families	______
copies	______	duties	______		

2 Rewrite the word in brackets. Change **y** to **i** and add **es**.

He (try) ______ to swim.

She (spy) ______ on people.

The (baby) ______ are crying.

The (city) ______ are large.

He (carry) ______ the bag.

3 Name it. Write the name for each.

f ______

b ______

c ______

Suffixes – adding es to words ending in y

4 Unscramble these list words.

rrcaies ______ bibaes ______

iesorst ______ iesarpt ______

iesrrwo ______ disesut ______

Challenge words

5 Copy each challenge word.

enemies ______ injuries ______

qualities ______ multiplies ______

properties ______ supplies ______

difficulties ______ factories ______

memories ______ libraries ______

6 Choose it. Circle and rewrite the correct word to complete the sentence.

The players had many [injuries] [injurys] after the game. ______

He is having [defficulties] [difficulties] with his computer. ______

There are big [factories] [faktories] in my town. ______

If he [multiples] [multiplies] six by two he will get twelve. ______

7 Alphabet. Write the challenge words in alphabetical order.

______ ______ ______

______ ______ ______

______ ______

______ ______

The j sound

1 Copy each list word.

gem	germ	jewel
jar	giant	adjust
jog	join	Japan
jug	June	magic
joke	July	energy
jump	angel	January
jelly	giraffe	

2 Name it. Write the name for each.

j ______ j ______ g ______ a ______

3 Sort.

The j sound

4 Complete each sentence with a list word.

We like to ______ on the trampoline.

The ___________ has a very long neck.

___________ is the first month of the year.

I poured everyone some juice from the ____.

The ________ wobbled on the plate.

Challenge words

5 Copy each challenge word.

urgent	____________	engine	____________
agile	____________	margin	____________
jigsaw	____________	juice	____________
allergy	____________	digit	____________
fragile	____________	jacket	____________

6 Interesting question. Answer the question with a challenge word.

What do you wear when it's cold? ____________

What is something that you can drink? ____________

What makes a car go? ____________

What game has puzzle pieces? ____________

What is another name for a single number? ____________

7 Write the challenge words in alphabetical order.

________ ________ ________ ________ ________

________ ________ ________ ________ ________

Word endings – le, el, al

1 Copy each list word.

angel	______	panel	______	title	______
oval	______	level	______	cruel	______
handle	______	camel	______	parcel	______
total	______	tunnel	______	dimple	______
novel	______	puddle	______	towel	______
noodle	______	signal	______	label	______
travel	______	kennel	______		

2 Sort the list words.

el

le

al

3 Name it. Write the name for each.

a ______

p ______

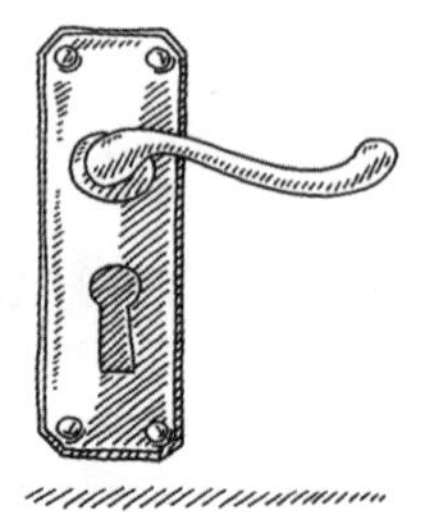

h ______

k ______

Word endings – le, el, al

4 Correct it. Write the word that is wrong correctly.

My grandparents sent me a parsel in the mail. ______

I jumped over the pudle. ______

I used a towl to dry off after my swim. ______

You can see her dimpl when she smiles. ______

I would like to travl to Africa one day. ______

Challenge words

5 Copy each challenge word.

turtle	______	shovel	______
buckle	______	cereal	______
people	______	capital	______
enamel	______	hospital	______
double	______	possible	______

6 Choose it. Circle and rewrite the correct word to complete the sentence.

Dad told us all to [buckle] [bukle] our seatbelts. ______

I helped [shoovel] [shovel] mulch onto the garden. ______

We ate [cereel] [cereal] for breakfast. ______

Lots of [people] [peeple] live in our town. ______

7 Word clues. Which challenge word matches?

twice the amount ______

a place where sick people are cared for ______

a reptile with a soft body and hard shell ______

the hard layer covering your teeth ______

Consonant digraph – wh

1 Copy each list word.

war	______	whip	______	worm	______
was	______	which	______	whale	______
wipe	______	witch	______	wheat	______
went	______	white	______	wheel	______
when	______	where	______	watch	______
what	______	world	______	while	______
wash	______	wall	______		

2 Unscramble the words. Write the word correctly.

The soldiers went to awr. ______

She uses shampoo to ashw her hair. ______

The snowy owl has hwite feathers. ______

The bird dug a romw out of the dirt. ______

I couldn't tell hwich pencil was mine. ______

3 The letter thief has left his bag behind! Put back the letters he stole.

wo _ _ _

wh _ _

w _ _ _

wh _ _ _

wi _ _ _

wh _ _ _

wa _ _

we _ _

Consonant digraph – wh

4 Name it. Write the name for each.

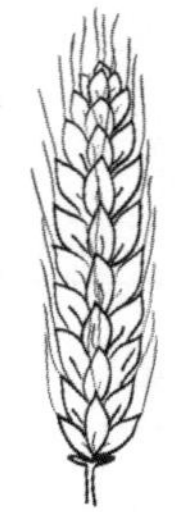
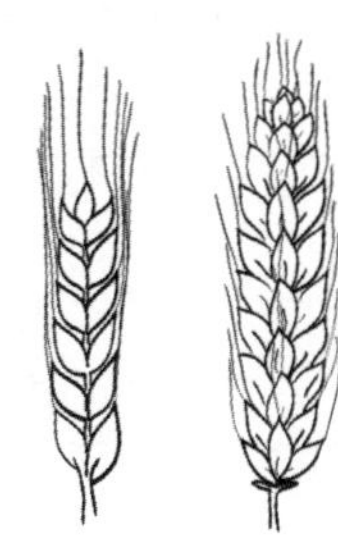
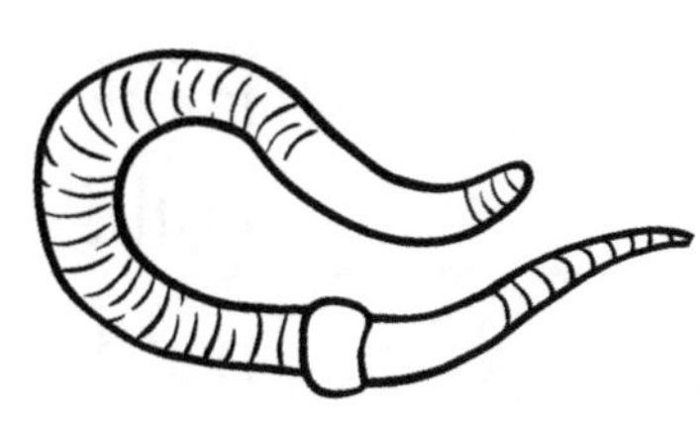

w ________ w ________ w ________ w ________

Challenge words

5 Copy each challenge word.

whistle	________	welcome	________
wagon	________	whether	________
whisk	________	weather	________
waste	________	wardrobe	________
whisker	________	wheeze	________

6 Complete the sentence with a challenge word.

She used a _ _ _ _ _ _ _ to whip the cream.

The _ _ _ _ _ _ _ was pulled by two strong horses.

I hung my clothes up in my _ _ _ _ _ _ _ _ _ _ _ .

The referee blew her _ _ _ _ _ _ _ _ _ _ to end the game.

They have predicted stormy _ _ _ _ _ _ _ _ _ _ all weekend.

7 Words within words. Make six new words with the letters in **wardrobe**.

________ ________ ________

________ ________ ________

Common exceptions words

1 Copy each list word.

door	______	past	______	father	______
poor	______	child	______	pretty	______
after	______	hold	______	half	______
even	______	sure	______	hour	______
who	______	sugar	______	grass	______
again	______	prove	______	climb	______
bath	______	great	______		

2 Complete each sentence with a list word.

I closed my bedroom d_ _ _ _ .

The charity helps p_ _ _ _ families.

We watch television a_ _ _ _ _ dinner.

Six and eight are e_ _ _ _ numbers.

I h_ _ _ _ Mum's hand when crossing the road.

3 Word clues. Which list word matches?

		g			makes food and drinks sweet
		u		▨	60 minutes
	a			▨	one of two equal parts of something
				d	a young person

Common exceptions words

4 Alphabet. Write the list words in alphabetical order.

Challenge words

5 Copy each challenge word.

because
behind
steak
beautiful
clothes
would
should
whole
improve
everybody

6 Underline the spelling mistake. Write the word correctly.

The chef poured gravy over the stek.
He thought her painting was butiful.
She ate a wole fruit bar.
He wished everibody would just get along.
We went shopping for new cloes.

7 Silly sentences. Use as many challenge words as possible to make a silly story.

Plurals – s, ves

1 Copy each list word.

lives ______	elves ______	loaves ______
puffs ______	waves ______	gloves ______
safes ______	stoves ______	giraffes ______
wives ______	leaves ______	cafes ______
reefs ______	sleeves ______	scarves ______
cliffs ______	olives ______	shelves ______
hives ______	wolves ______	

2 **More than one.** Write the singular and plural for each word.

	______	______	
	______	______	
	______	______	
	______	______	

3 Write the word in brackets correctly.

I wear (glove) ______ to keep my hands warm.

We saw lots of (giraffe) ______ at the zoo.

There are three (shelf) ______ in the cupboard.

There are many (cafe) ______ near us.

Plurals – s, ves

4 Sort it.

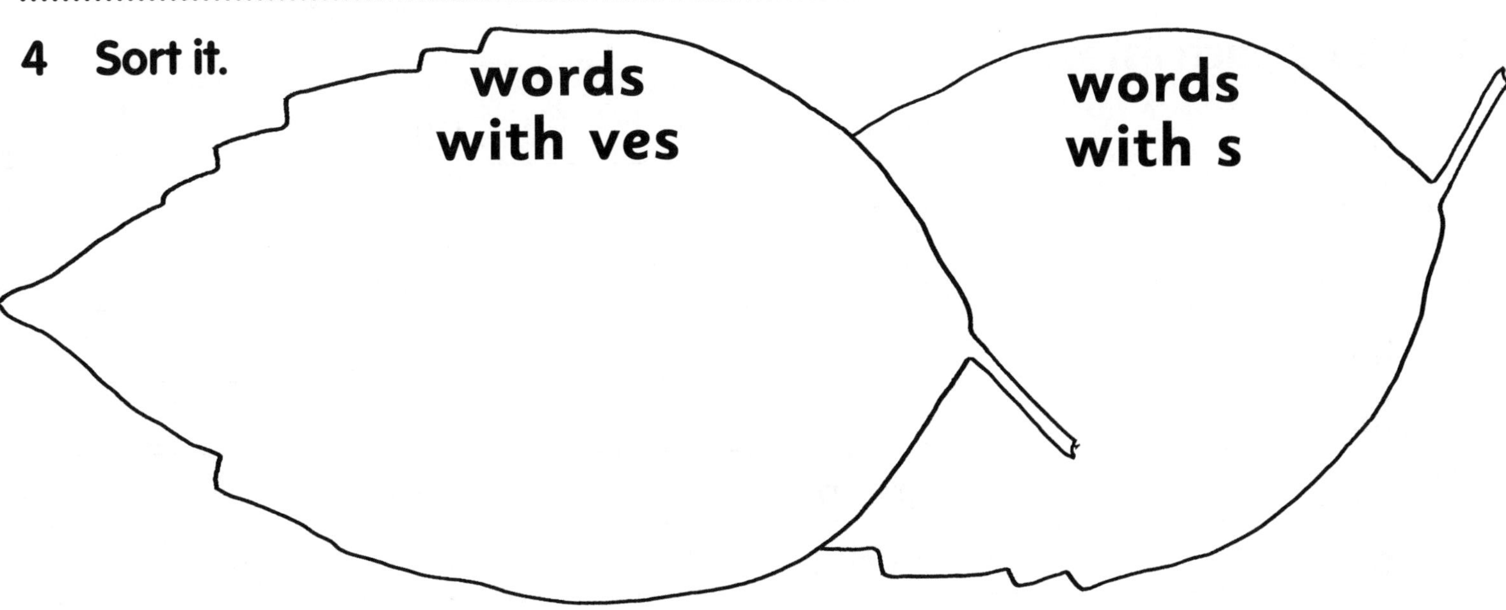

Challenge words

5 Copy each challenge word.

knives	________	calves	________
halves	________	grooves	________
sheaves	________	selves	________
thieves	________	flagstaffs	________
nerves	________	detectives	________

6 Complete the sentence with a challenge word.

In the cutlery drawer we have spoons, forks and ________.

We saw lots of ________ with their mothers on the farm.

My shoes have ________ on the bottom.

I cut the orange into two ________.

7 Silly sentences. Use as many challenge words as possible to make a silly story.

____

____

Vowel sounds – long oo exceptions

1 Copy each list word.

you ____	rude ____	threw ____
fruit ____	grew ____	blew ____
shoe ____	clue ____	chew ____
blue ____	crew ____	screw ____
flew ____	suit ____	prune ____
soup ____	group ____	ruby ____
true ____	truth ____	

2 Name.

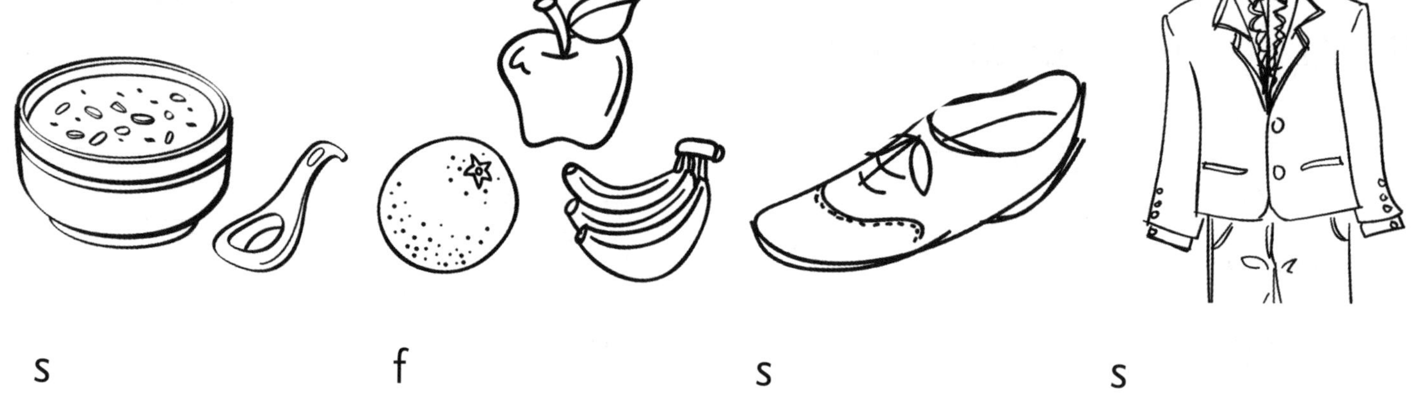

s ____ f ____ s ____ s ____

3 Match the clue to a list word.

	u			//////	a deep red gem
		o		//////	something worn on your foot
f					grown on trees
	r			e	a dried plum
		u		//////	the colour of the sky

Vowel sounds – long oo exceptions

4 Missing letters. Write the missing letters.

sc__ __ __ th__ __ __
cr__ __ gr__ __
ch__ __ fl__ __
cl__ __ s__ __p
bl__ __ r__d__

Challenge words

5 Copy each challenge word.

bruise ________ should ________
bluish ________ through ________
cruise ________ canoe ________
would ________ cashew ________
could ________ gruesome ________

6 Choose it. Circle and rewrite the correct word to complete the sentence.

I [could] [cowld] not stop listening to her new song. ________
I screamed as my brother capsized our [canoo] [canoe]. ________
The movie was too [groosome] [gruesome] to watch. ________
The train sped [throo] [through] the tunnel. ________

7 Complete the sentence with a challenge word.

I had a large ________ on my leg after falling over.
I had a packet of ________ nuts for my morning snack.
I wish that I ________ fly like a bird.
Mum told me that I ________ go and clean my room.

Suffixes – ful, less

1 Copy each list word.

awful ______	handful ______	grateful ______
useless ______	joyful ______	powerful ______
helpful ______	playful ______	spiteful ______
careless ______	mouthful ______	cheerful ______
spoonful ______	graceful ______	truthful ______
plateful ______	thankful ______	harmless ______
restless ______	forgetful ______	

2 Sort.

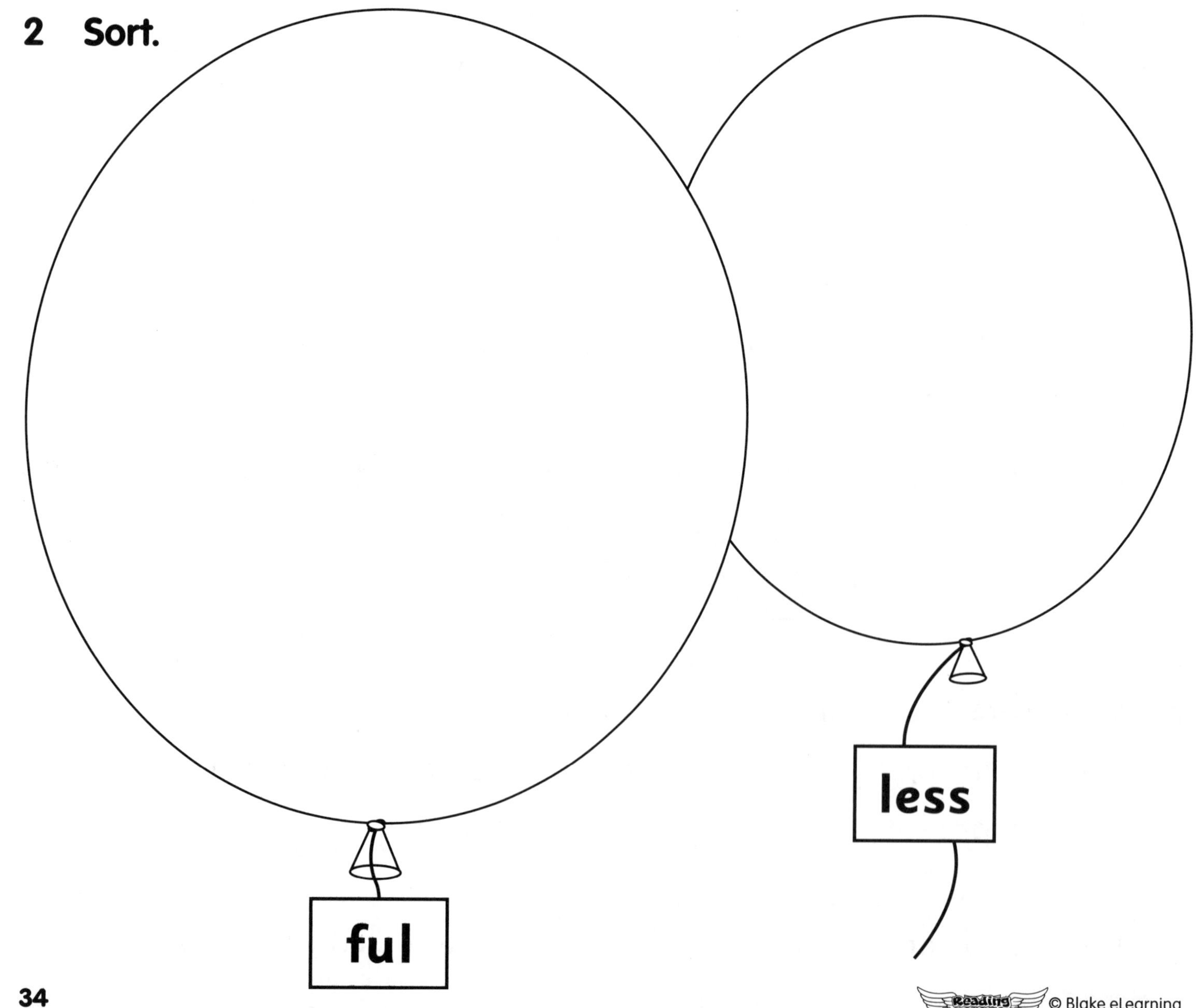

Suffixes – ful, less

3 Underline the spelling mistakes. Write the word correctly.

She would only eat a spoonfull of the soup. ____________

Dad gave us each a platefull of pasta. ____________

His careles mistake got him into trouble. ____________

Mum told us she wanted a truthfull answer. ____________

Challenge words

4 Copy each challenge word.

beautiful	____________	merciful	____________
wonderful	____________	plentiful	____________
colourless	____________	houseful	____________
delightful	____________	peaceful	____________
faithful	____________	disgraceful	____________

5 Complete the sentence with a list word.

We had a p____________ supply of firewood.

Water is a c____________ liquid.

The teacher said I had made w____________ progress this year.

She thought their behaviour was d____________ .

6 Silly sentences. Use as many challenge words as possible to make a silly story.

____

____

____

Consonant digraphs – kn, gn, wr

1 Copy each list word.

know	____________	wreck	____________	knack	____________
gnat	____________	write	____________	gnome	____________
knee	____________	knot	____________	wrong	____________
wrap	____________	knife	____________	wrote	____________
knit	____________	knock	____________	wrist	____________
knob	____________	kneel	____________	gnash	____________
knew	____________	knelt	____________		

2 Name.

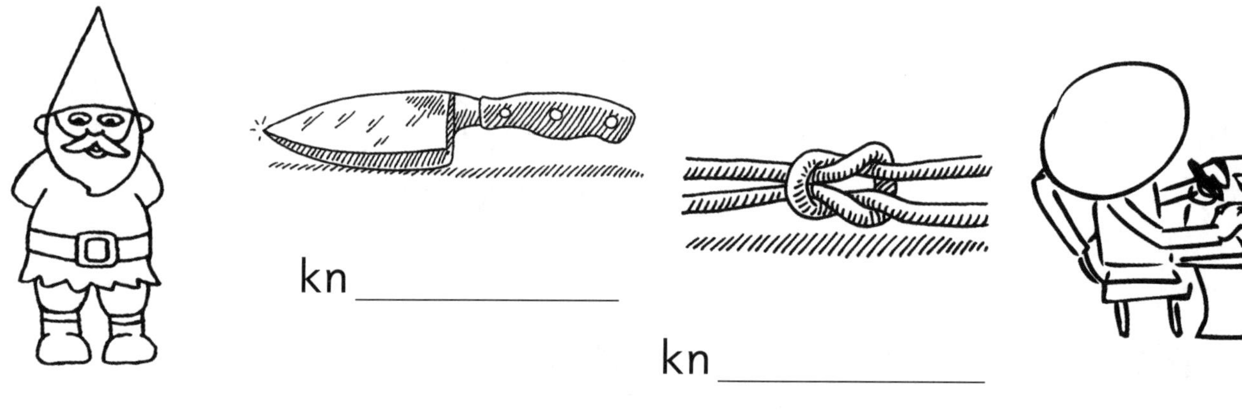

gn ____________ kn ____________ kn ____________ wr ____________

3 Make the words fit the blocks.

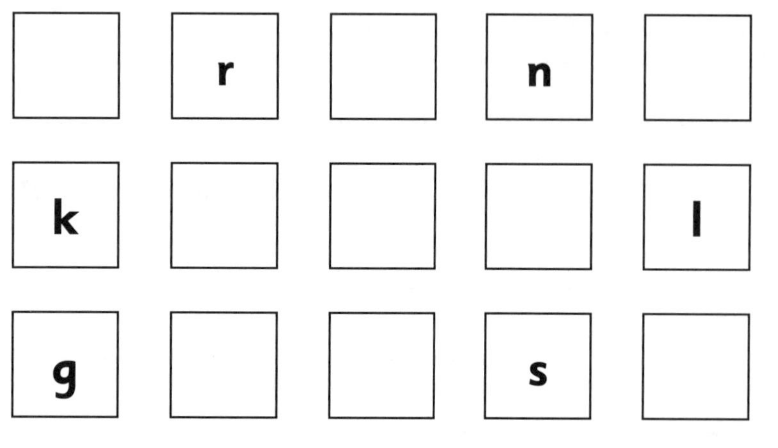

Consonant digraphs – kn, gn, wr

4 Complete each sentence with a list word.

I heard a ________ at the front door.

I ________ down to tie my shoelaces.

I had trouble brushing the ______ out of my hair.

I hooked the bracelet around my ________.

Challenge words

5 Copy each challenge word.

written	______________	wrestle	______________
wreckage	______________	knight	______________
knuckle	______________	known	______________
wrinkle	______________	gnaw	______________
wriggle	______________	knead	______________

6 Complete the sentence with a challenge word.

I could not get the ring over my ___________.

I watched the worm ___________ in the dirt.

The brave __________ rode away on his horse.

The _____________ from the storm took weeks to clean up.

The baker must ________ the dough before putting it in the oven.

7 Silly sentences. Use as many challenge words as possible to make a silly story.

____

____

____

Suffixes – er, est

1 Copy each list word.

paler ______	neatest ______	prouder ______
duller ______	cuter ______	steeper ______
nicer ______	newest ______	fullest ______
fewer ______	whiter ______	sharper ______
finest ______	coldest ______	smallest ______
later ______	thickest ______	clearest ______
loudest ______	fresher ______	

2 Sort it.

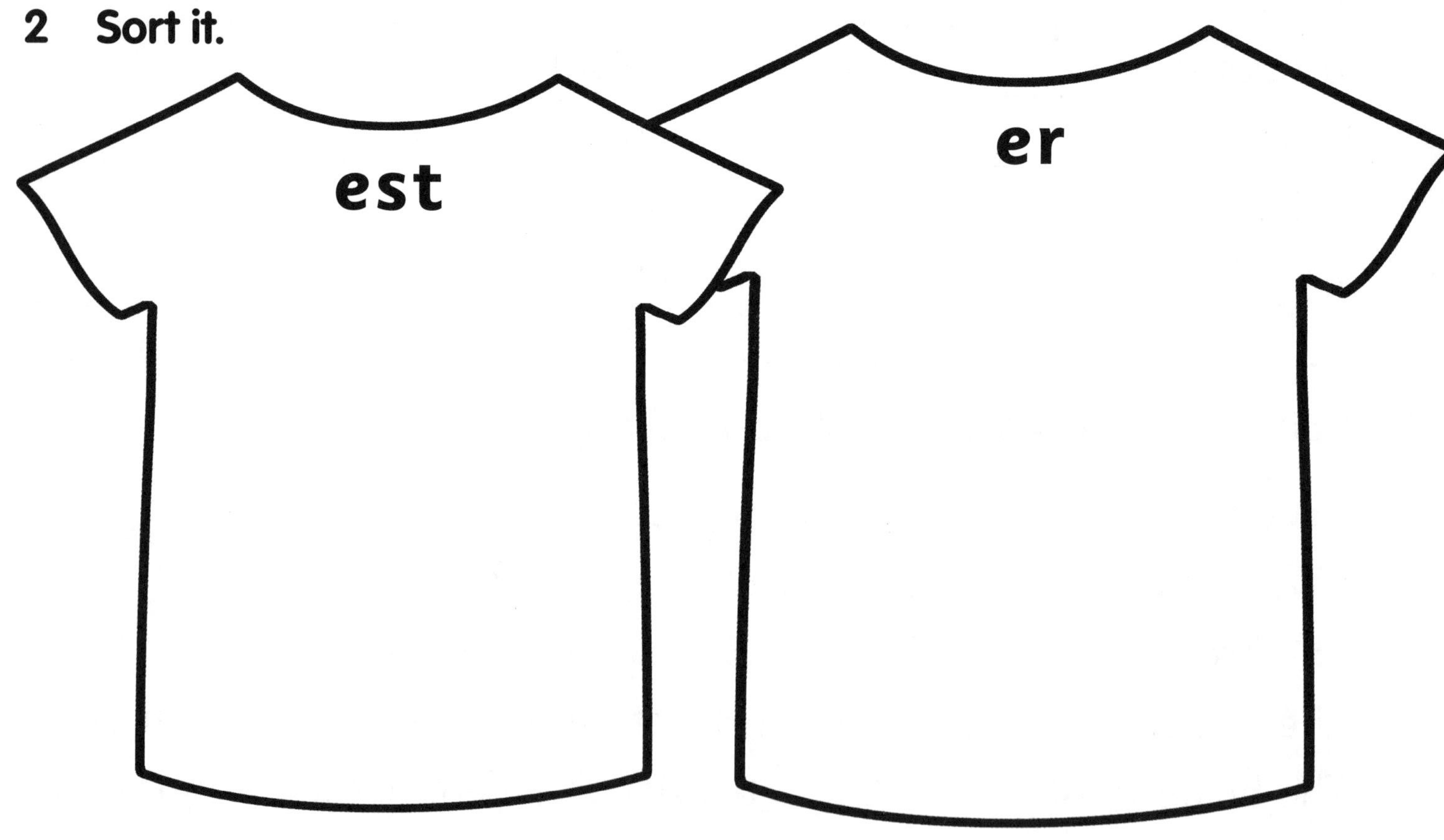

3 Correct it. Write the word that is wrong correctly.

Kay chose the smalest slice of cake. ______

I think my puppy is coouter than hers. ______

The mountain was a lot steper than it looked. ______

Suffixes – er, est

4 Word shapes. Match these list words to their word shapes.

neatest **fresher** **paler** **sharper** **nicer**

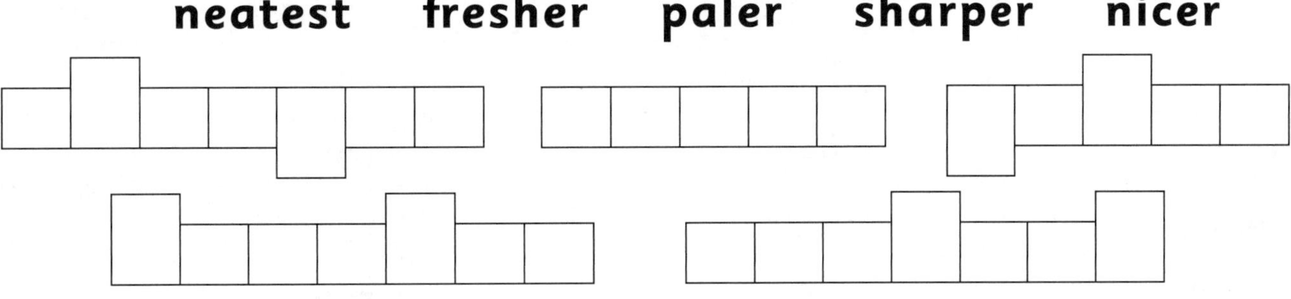

Challenge words

5 Copy each challenge word.

higher ______	straighter ______
bluer ______	quietest ______
narrowest ______	younger ______
gentler ______	looser ______
brightest ______	fiercer ______

6 Choose it. Circle and rewrite the correct word to complete the sentence.

I am [yunger] [younger] than my brother. ______

The sun is [britest] [brightest] at midday. ______

Her hair is a lot [straighter] [streighter] than my hair. ______

The [fiercer] [fierser] warrior won the battle. ______

The bird flew [higher] [heigher] than the trees. ______

7 Silly sentences. Use as many challenge words as possible to make a silly story.

______

______

______

Homophones

1 Copy each list word.

sale ______	steal ______	sight ______
sail ______	flee ______	site ______
meet ______	flea ______	toe ______
meat ______	hole ______	tow ______
plane ______	whole ______	rain ______
plain ______	pray ______	rein ______
steel ______	prey ______	

2 Circle the right word.

Picture	Words	Picture	Words	Picture	Words
	flea flee		hole whole		tow toe
	plane plain		sail sale		rein rain
	meet meat		steel steal		

3 Missing word.

The ________ landed safely at the airport.

The wombat dug a deep ______ in the dirt.

We watched the boats ______ past the harbour.

I bought a box of old toys at the garage ______.

My brother tried to ________ my new game.

Homophones

4 Word clues. Which word matches?

a tiny jumping insect that bites ______

leather straps that help a rider control a horse ______

a hard, strong metal ______

to run away or escape ______

an animal that is hunted by another ______

Challenge words

5 Copy each challenge word.

wear	______	haul	______
where	______	rays	______
hire	______	raise	______
higher	______	morning	______
hall	______	mourning	______

6 Choose it. Circle and rewrite the correct word to complete the sentence.

I eat breakfast in the [morning] [mourning]. ______

We enjoyed the warmth of the sun's [raise] [rays]. ______

We climbed [higher] [hire] up the tree. ______

They have school assemblies in the big [haul] [hall]. ______

I didn't know [where] [wear] my sister was hiding. ______

7 Silly sentences. Use as many challenge words as possible to make a silly story.

______

______

______

Suffixes – ing, ed

1 Copy each list word.

rubbed ____________	rammed ____________	grabbed ____________
jogging ____________	bobbing ____________	stopped ____________
jogged ____________	tipped ____________	trapping ____________
wagging ____________	thinned ____________	blotted ____________
sagged ____________	planned ____________	skinned ____________
sipped ____________	stabbed ____________	flopped ____________
stopping ____________	gripping ____________	

2 Sort.

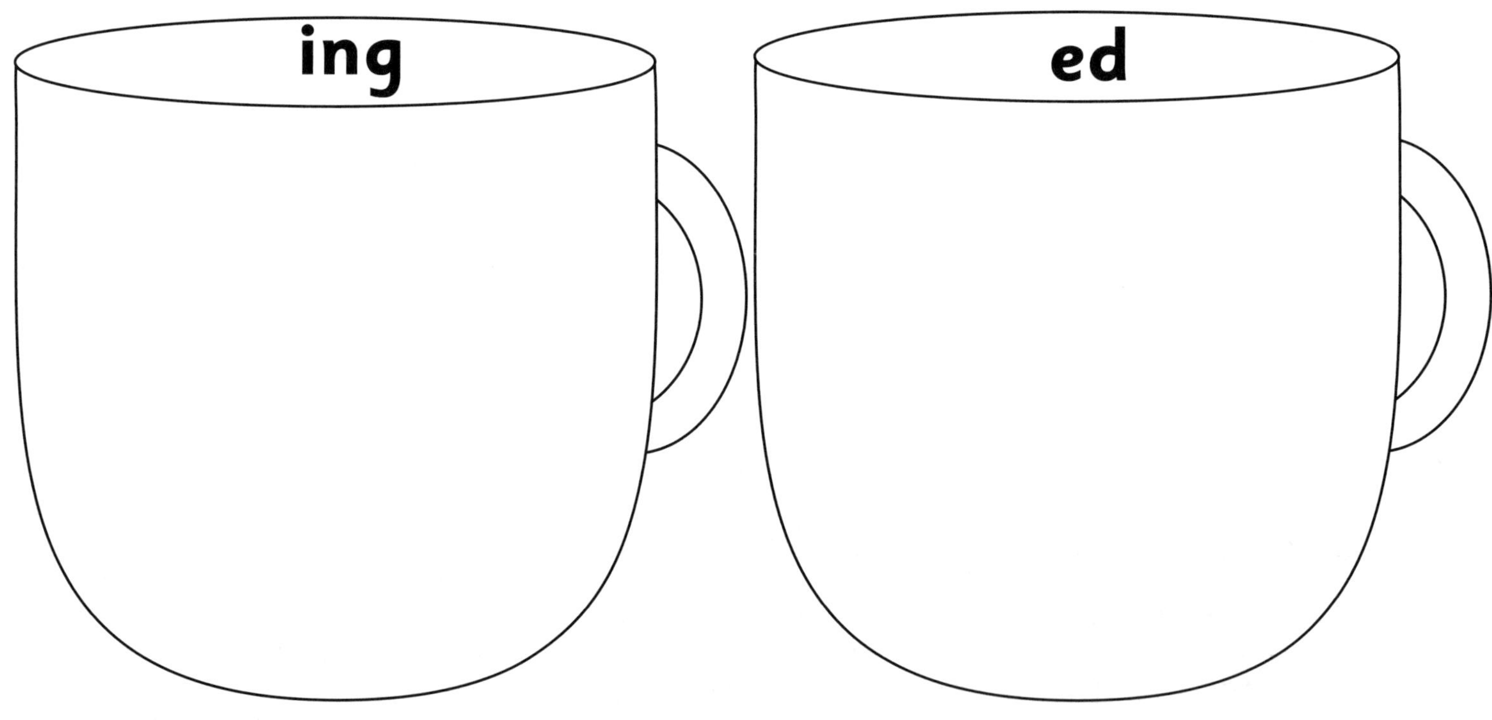

3 Complete each sentence with a list word.

The soccer team is ___________ around the oval.

Yesterday, my team ___________ around the oval.

I ___________ the monkey bars tightly so I wouldn't fall.

The boats are ___________ on the water.

Suffixes – ing, ed

Challenge words

4 Copy each challenge word.

prodding ____________________

stunned ____________________

scanning ____________________

shipped ____________________

knitting ____________________

throbbed ____________________

strapping ____________________

shrugged ____________________

scrubbing ____________________

squatted ____________________

5 Choose it. Circle and rewrite the correct word to complete the sentence.

We [shiped] [shipped] the package across the country. __________

Grandma is [knitting] [kniting] a big woolly jumper. __________

My knee [throbbed] [throbed] with pain after I fell over. __________

I was [stuned] [stunned] when my name was called out. __________

She [squatted] [squated] down beside me to take a closer look. __________

6 Hidden words. Find the challenge word.

sdjfscanningsggf ____________________

dfsshruggedgvsf ____________________

dgvsscrubbingdfj ____________________

sdfstrappingdfdfs ____________________

ersproddinggfdre ____________________

The k sound – k, ck

1 Copy each list word.

beak ______	luck ______	mask ______
bank ______	dusk ______	stick ______
lock ______	peck ______	shack ______
tank ______	track ______	stock ______
rock ______	pluck ______	speak ______
pink ______	cheek ______	trunk ______
tick ______	check ______	

2 Name.

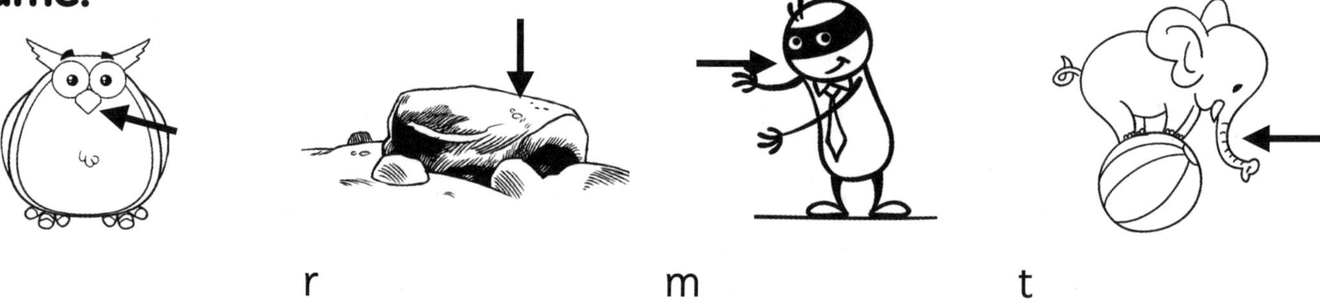

b ______ r ______ m ______ t ______

3 Sort it.

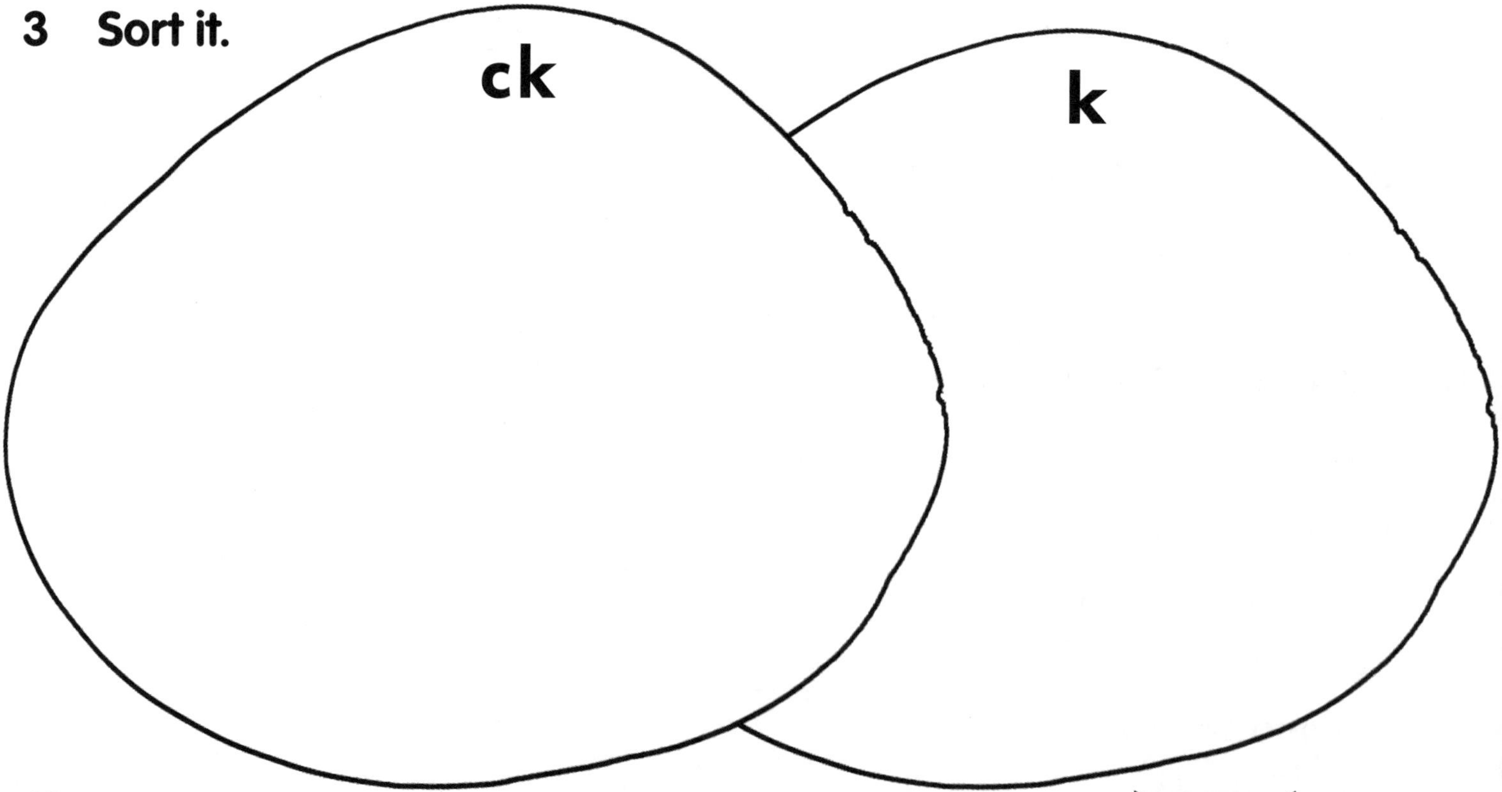

ck

k

The k sound – k, ck

4 **Word clues.** Which list word matches?

a place to save and borrow money ______

the colour of a flamingo ______

the time of day just before night ______

Challenge words

5 **Copy each challenge word.**

soak ______

cloak ______

thank ______

crook ______

streak ______

stork ______

struck ______

attack ______

paddock ______

chipmunk ______

6 **Interesting question.** Answer the question with a challenge word.

Where are sheep kept? ______

What bird has very long legs? ______

What is an animal like a squirrel? ______

What's another word for thief? ______

7 **Complete the sentence with a challenge word.**

I like to ______ in a hot bath after a long day.

I made sure to ______ her for my birthday present.

We rode the horses around the ______.

The ______ was collecting nuts for the winter.

Suffixes – ly

1 Copy each list word.

badly ______	mainly ______	largely ______
slowly ______	softly ______	swiftly ______
nicely ______	clearly ______	gently ______
suddenly ______	quickly ______	firmly ______
mostly ______	happily ______	quietly ______
strongly ______	easily ______	fairly ______
shyly ______	calmly ______	

2 Complete the table. Use a list word to complete the table.

bad	badly
quick	
strong	
most	
nice	

3 Correct it. Write the word that is wrong correctly.

I jumped easly over the low fence. ______

I quikly ate my dinner so I could play outside. ______

We spoke sofly so we didn't wake our parents. ______

I sudenly had a brilliant idea. ______

The turtle crawled slowlee up the beach. ______

Suffixes – ly

4 Write the list words in alphabetical order.

Challenge words

5 Copy each challenge word.

extremely		completely	
actually		differently	
finally		surely	
slightly		absolutely	
normally		equally	

6 Choose it. Circle and rewrite the correct word to complete the sentence.

Mum shared the food | eqwually | equally | between us. ______

I | finaly | finally | finished my art project. ______

We went in | completly | completely | different directions. ______

I am | slightly | sleightly | taller than my friend. ______

7 Silly sentences. Use as many challenge words as possible to make a silly story.

Word endings – ge

1 Copy each list word.

age ______	hedge ______	strange ______
edge ______	fudge ______	change ______
huge ______	wedge ______	fringe ______
village ______	bridge ______	smudge ______
badge ______	image ______	garage ______
large ______	orange ______	plunge ______
judge ______	charge ______	

2 Name it. Write the name for each.

b ______

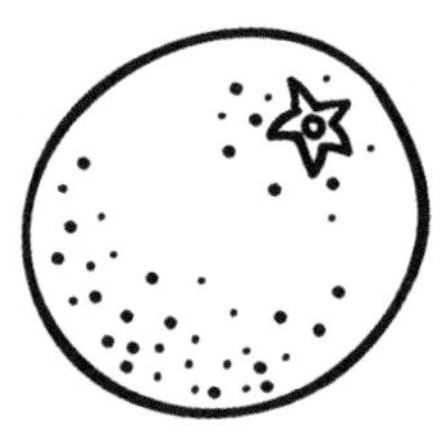

o ______

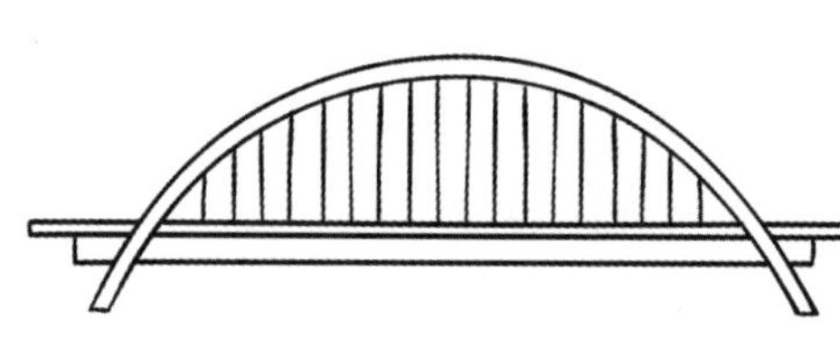

b ______

h ______

j ______

3 Word clues. Which list word matches?

a dirty mark or stain ______

unusual or odd ______

a picture of something ______

a round, juicy fruit ______

a row of bushes used as a fence ______

Word endings – ge

4 Unscramble it. Unscramble the letters to make a list word.

ungple ______ ngecha ______
ingefr ______ agevill ______
rgecha ______ raggae ______

Challenge words

5 Copy each challenge word.

bulge ______ partridge ______
cottage ______ sausage ______
package ______ damage ______
passage ______ manage ______
cringe ______ courage ______

6 Word clues. Which challenge word matches?

a small house ______
a box used to transport something ______
the ability to face your fears ______
a medium-sized bird ______
thin tube of minced meat ______

7 Choose it. Circle the correct challenge word to complete the sentence.

We apologised for the [damage] [damge] we did to the garden.
We could see a light at the end of the dark [pasage] [passage].
I walked to the post office to collect my [package] [pakage].
I always [cringe] [crenge] at the sound of sirens.

Compound words

1 Copy each list word.

armpit	______	windmill	______	eyebrow	______
pancake	______	raincoat	______	handshake	______
freeway	______	snowman	______	rainfall	______
starfish	______	backpack	______	leftovers	______
shoelace	______	grandchild	______	teardrop	______
anybody	______	hairbrush	______	strawberry	______
uphill	______	driveway	______		

2 **Picture words.** Add the pictures to make a list word.

Compound words

4 Underline the spelling mistakes. Write the word correctly.

Strawbery is my favourite flavour of ice-cream. ____________

I want it to snow so that I can build a snoman. ____________

On rainy days I pack my umbrella and raincote. ____________

I packed my books and pencil case into my bakpack. ____________

I couldn't find my harebrush, so I had to use my comb. ____________

Challenge words

5 Copy each challenge word.

outdoors	____________	background	____________
marketplace	____________	doughnut	____________
elsewhere	____________	clockwork	____________
downstairs	____________	earphone	____________
watermelon	____________	cheeseburger	____________

6 Complete the sentence with a challenge word.

When I eat ____________ I always spit out the black seeds.

Dad told us to go and play ____________.

We brought home a huge box of peaches from the ____________.

I wanted the ____________ with pink icing and sprinkles.

I pulled my ____________ out so I could hear what she was saying.

7 Word clues. Which challenge word matches?

a large fruit with green skin ____________

describes something running smoothly ____________

an area where goods are sold ____________

Contractions

1 Copy each list word.

I'm ______	we'll ______	hasn't ______
he's ______	don't ______	where's ______
it's ______	she'll ______	what's ______
I've ______	it'd ______	you'd ______
how's ______	who's ______	can't ______
there's ______	it'll ______	didn't ______
won't ______	who'll ______	

2 Correct it. Write the word that is wrong correctly.

Jay told me that h'es not coming to the party. ______

I cant' stand on my head! ______

Don't worry, she'l be here any minute. ______

Im the tallest person in my class. ______

I'ts been two weeks since the holidays ended. ______

3 Match. Draw a line to match the words to their contractions.

has not	didn't
where is	hasn't
did not	how's
I have	where's
how is	I've

Contractions

4 Missing apostrophe. Rewrite the word with the apostrophe in the correct place.

itll ______ wont ______ well ______ youd ______

Challenge words

5 Copy each challenge word.

wasn't ______	haven't ______
they've ______	doesn't ______
you're ______	o'clock ______
mustn't ______	couldn't ______
weren't ______	would've ______

6 Meaning. Which list word means?

were not ______	would have ______
does not ______	was not ______
could not ______	you are ______

7 Choose it. Circle and rewrite the correct word to complete the sentence.

I [wasn't] [wan'st] sure which direction we should take. ______

You [musun't] [mustn't] make a sound or you'll wake the baby. ______

I [couldn't] [could't] go to soccer practice because I felt unwell. ______

School starts promptly at nine [o'clock] [oclock]. ______

Making plurals – adding s and es

1 Copy each list word.

pigs ______	cages ______	classes ______
bees ______	eyes ______	flashes ______
foxes ______	lions ______	bunches ______
dishes ______	tricks ______	kisses ______
books ______	things ______	sharks ______
rocks ______	plants ______	lambs ______
coats ______	spiders ______	

2 More than one. Write the singular and plural for each word.

	______	______	
	______	______	
	______	______	
	______	______	
	______	______	
	______	______	
	______	______	
	______	______	

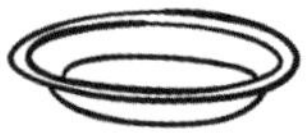

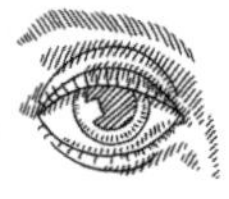

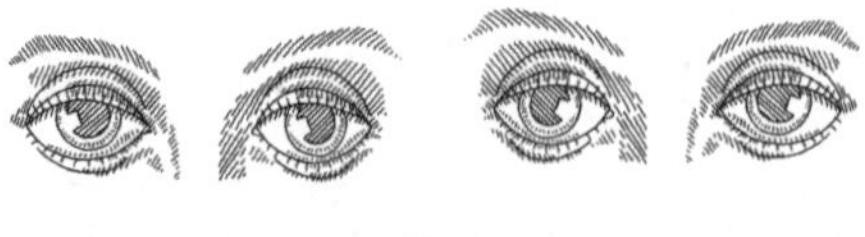

Making plurals – adding s and es

3 Complete each sentence with a list word.

There were two __________ rolling in the mud.

We could hear the __________ roaring loudly outside our tent.

I watched several __________ buzzing noisily around the garden.

I hung all the __________ in the closet.

I borrowed two new __________ from the library.

The florist had __________ of beautiful flowers outside her shop.

Challenge words

4 Copy each challenge word.

fingers	__________	branches	__________
flowers	__________	quizzes	__________
monkeys	__________	oranges	__________
catches	__________	giraffes	__________
watches	__________	cabbages	__________

5 Interesting question. Answer the question with a challenge word.

What kinds of animals have long necks? __________

What do bees collect pollen from? __________

What do you have on your hands? __________

What fruit has the same name and colour? __________

6 Complete the sentence.

The __________ sat in the tree eating bananas.

I have five __________ on one hand and five toes on one foot.

I picked seven juicy __________ from the tree.

Irregular verbs – past tense

1 Copy each list word.

did ______	awoke ______	forgot ______
ate ______	became ______	froze ______
fled ______	began ______	swung ______
gave ______	bound ______	flung ______
went ______	clung ______	fought ______
stole ______	sprang ______	chose ______
shook ______	knew ______	

2 Unscramble it. Unscramble these list words.

mecabe ______	undbo ______
ngaspr ______	ghtfou ______
ungsw ______	okeaw ______

3 Missing letters. Write the missing letters.

d _ d cl _ _ g ch _ _ e _ ne _ s _ _ l _

4 Correct it. Write the word in brackets correctly.

I [awake] in the middle of the night. ______

After his bath the dog [shake] water everywhere. ______

Yesterday I [eat] five sandwiches and two muesli bars. ______

Mum [give] me some money to buy bread. ______

I [forget] to pack my overdue library books. ______

Irregular verbs – past tense

Challenge words

5 Copy each challenge word.

built	______	caught	______
brought	______	dealt	______
taught	______	heard	______
struck	______	meant	______
shrank	______	understood	______

6 Choose it. Circle and rewrite the correct word to complete the sentence.

I [bringed] [brought] chocolate brownies to the class party.

______

I [taught] [teached] my little sister how to count to five.

______

The branch [struck] [strikeed] me in the back of the head. ______

I hoped that she [understood] [understand] my instructions. ______

I [caught] [catched] the ball before it hit the window. ______

7 Silly sentences. Use as many challenge words as possible to make a silly story.

______

______

______

Split digraphs – a-e, e-e, i-e, o-e, u-e

1 Copy each list word.

face	______	stone	______	prune	______
safe	______	smile	______	slide	______
nine	______	rule	______	skate	______
bone	______	alone	______	blade	______
June	______	stole	______	shade	______
these	______	glide	______	whole	______
close	______	plate	______		

2 Name it. Write the name for each.

s ______ p ______ b ______ n ______

3 In a group. Write the list word that belongs in each group.

skeleton, skin, ______

grin, laugh, ______

bowl, cup, ______

rock, pebble, ______

knife, sword, ______

seven, eight, ______

4 Complete the table. Sort each list word into a column.

a-e	e-e	i-e	o-e	u-e

Split digraphs – a-e, e-e, i-e, o-e, u-e

Challenge words

5 Copy each challenge word.

scrape ____________
while ____________
shave ____________
tadpole ____________
gnome ____________
whale ____________
guide ____________
lemonade ____________
microwave ____________
crocodile ____________

6 Interesting question. Answer the question with a challenge word.

What reptile has large snapping jaws with lots of sharp teeth? ____________

What drink can you make with lemons, sugar and water? ____________

What is a young frog called? ____________

What animal lives underwater and breathes through its blowhole? ____________

What can you use to heat up food? ____________

7 Complete the sentence with a challenge word.

I had to ____________ the melted cheese off the pan.

Dad uses an electric razor to ____________ his face.

The ____________ had started to grow long legs.

Grandma bought a new ____________ for her garden.

Vowel digraphs – ea, ee

1 Copy each list word.

meet ______	beat ______	pleat ______
meat ______	sheet ______	wheat ______
feet ______	neat ______	bleat ______
heat ______	treat ______	upbeat ______
greet ______	sweet ______	street ______
seat ______	cheat ______	repeat ______
fleet ______	tweet ______	

2 Sort.

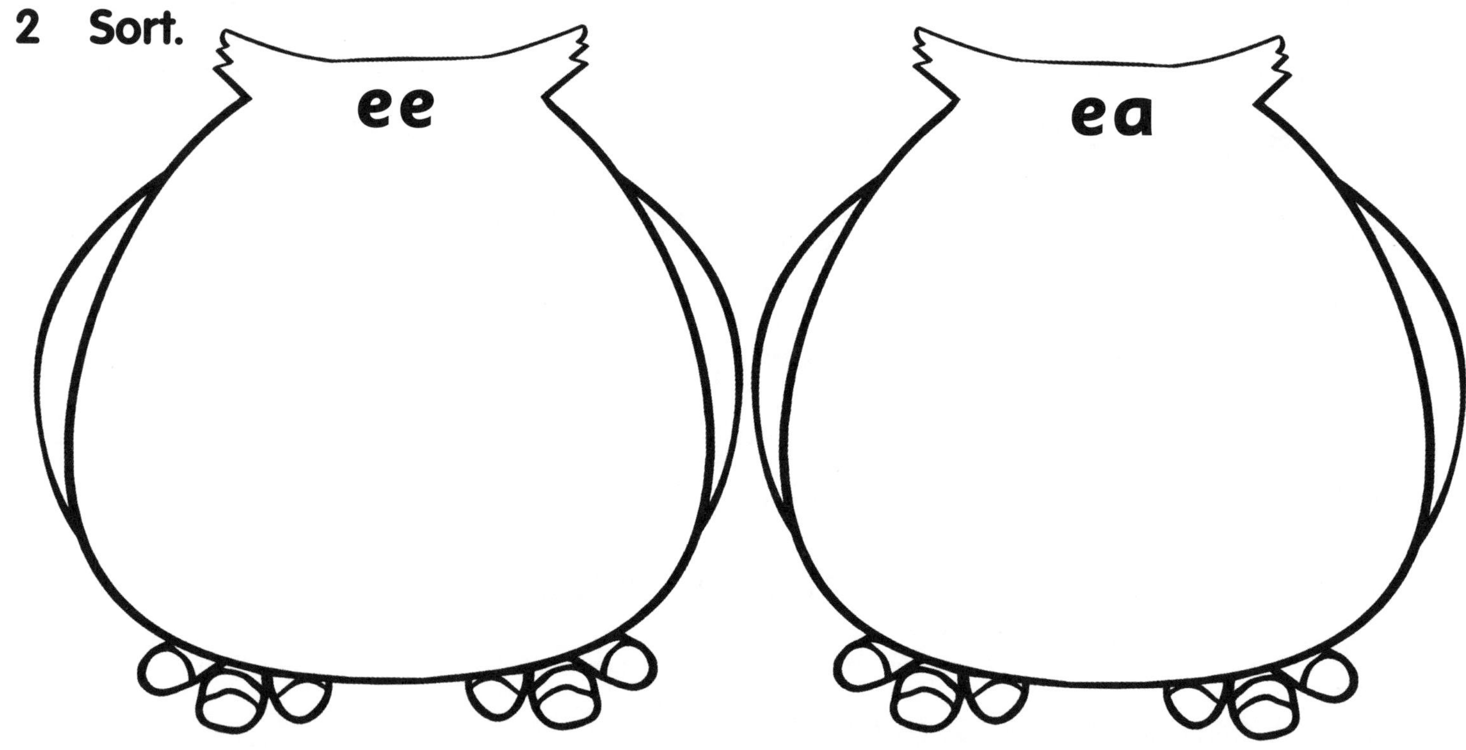

3 Complete each sentence with a list word.

I opened the door to ____________ our visitors.

In summer I only need a light ____________ on my bed.

I couldn't find my shoes, so I ran to the shops in bare ____________.

My friend and I live on the same ____________.

We played in the ____________ of the summer day.

Vowel digraphs – ea, ee

4 Meaning. Which list word means?

a group of ships ______________________

the sound made by a goat or sheep ______________________

to defeat a person ______________________

the sound made by a bird ______________________

a grain used to make flour ______________________

Challenge words

5 Copy each challenge word.

compete	______________	lorikeet	______________
delete	______________	retreat	______________
defeat	______________	complete	______________
overeat	______________	concrete	______________
athlete	______________	heartbeat	______________

6 Word clues. Which challenge word matches?

to eat too much ______________________

to move back or away from something ______________________

someone who participates in sports ______________________

a small brightly coloured parrot ______________________

7 Choose it. Circle the correct challenge word to complete the sentence.

I decided not to [compete] [compet] in this year's fun run.

I ran a [complet] [complete] circuit of the oval.

The doctor listened to my [heartbeat] [hertbeat].

Word endings – ar, er, or

1 Copy each list word.

sugar ______	gather ______	cracker ______
butter ______	number ______	saucer ______
doctor ______	pepper ______	wander ______
finger ______	dollar ______	tractor ______
enter ______	brother ______	together ______
dinner ______	mirror ______	another ______
spider ______	Easter ______	

2 Name.

t ______ s ______ d ______ s ______

3 **In a group.** Write the list word that belongs in each group.

lunch, breakfast, ______

biscuit, cookie, ______

sister, mother, ______

plate, dish, ______

hand, palm, ______

field, crops, ______

4 **Unscramble it.** Unscramble the letters to make a list word.

teren ______

thertoge ______

rormir ______

therano ______

derwan ______

perpep ______

Word endings – ar, er, or

5 Correct it. Write the word that is wrong correctly.

The docttor gave Isha some medicine. ____________

Michael set the salt and peper on the table. ____________

I found a dolar coin in the pocket of my jeans. ____________

I found him looking at his reflection in the miror. ____________

We were told not to wandr off without supervision. ____________

Challenge words

6 Copy each challenge word.

answer	____________	October	____________
feather	____________	November	____________
deliver	____________	cellar	____________
lawyer	____________	alligator	____________
September	____________	caterpillar	____________

7 Solve it. Read the clue and complete the sentence.

I look like a crocodile. I am an ____________.

August is before me and October is after me. I am ____________.

I am the second last month of the year. I am ____________.

I am found on birds. I am a ____________.

I will turn into a butterfly one day. I am a ____________.

8 Silly sentences. Use as many list words as possible to make a silly story.

____

____

____

Vowel sounds – ai, a-e

1 Copy each list word.

parade ______	grade ______	upgrade ______
paid ______	blade ______	afraid ______
made ______	raid ______	decade ______
wade ______	aid ______	invade ______
maid ______	trade ______	arcade ______
laid ______	shade ______	sunshade ______
fade ______	spade ______	

2 Meaning. Which list word means?

a woman paid to do housework ______

ten years ______

a tool used for digging ______

to give help to someone in need ______

a sudden surprise attack ______

3 Missing letters. Write the missing letters.

in _ _ d _	b _ _ de	wad _
sunsh _ _ _	tra _ _	ar _ _ d _

4 Write the list words in alphabetical order.

Vowel sounds – ai, a-e

Challenge words

5 Copy each challenge word.

cascade ____________________

braid ____________________

unafraid ____________________

grenade ____________________

mermaid ____________________

lemonade ____________________

bridesmaid ____________________

persuade ____________________

repaid ____________________

marmalade ____________________

6 Choose it. Circle and rewrite the correct word to complete the sentence.

I plaited her long hair into a [braid] [breid] . ____________________

Tim spread [marmelade] [marmalade] on his toast. ____________________

My sister will be a [bridesmeid] [bridesmaid] at our cousin's wedding. ____________________

I poured everyone a cool glass of [lemonaid] [lemonade].

____

Hannah tried to [persuade] [pursade] her mother to buy ice-cream.

____

7 Silly sentences. Use as many challenge words as possible to make a silly story.

____

____

____

Word building

1 Copy each list word.

law	______	fright	______
lawful	______	frighten	______
unlawful	______	frightened	______
try	______	happily	______
trying	______	happiness	______
tried	______	happiest	______
watch	______	begin	______
watching	______	beginning	______
watched	______	beginner	______
watchful	______	began	______

2 Word building. Add suffixes to build words.

try	fright	begin

3 Complete the sentence with a list word.

The thief was arrested for breaking the ______.

It is ______ to steal from other people.

The loud thunder gave me a ______.

I am ______ of tight spaces.

My brother is ______ cartoons in the lounge room.

Word building

4 Unscramble it. Unscramble the letters to make a list word.

chedwat __________

inesshapp __________

innerbeg __________

chfulwat __________

inningbeg __________

Challenge words

5 Copy each challenge word.

garden __________

gardening __________

gardener __________

decide __________

deciding __________

decision __________

friend __________

friendly __________

friendliness __________

unfriendly __________

6 Word clues. Which challenge word matches?

Lin is helping plant vegetables in the school __________.

Shay and Olly are still __________ which movie to see.

The __________ was not happy with the state of her roses.

The new girl seemed to be very __________.

I couldn't __________ which book I liked better.

7 Silly sentences. Use as many challenge words as possible to make a silly story.

____

____

____

Suffixes – er, est

1 Copy each list word.

bigger	______	dimmer	______
biggest	______	dirtier	______
flatter	______	dirtiest	______
tinier	______	tidier	______
tiniest	______	fittest	______
easier	______	funnier	______
easiest	______	funniest	______
saddest	______	smelliest	______
busiest	______	heavier	______
smallest	______	heaviest	______

2 Sort.

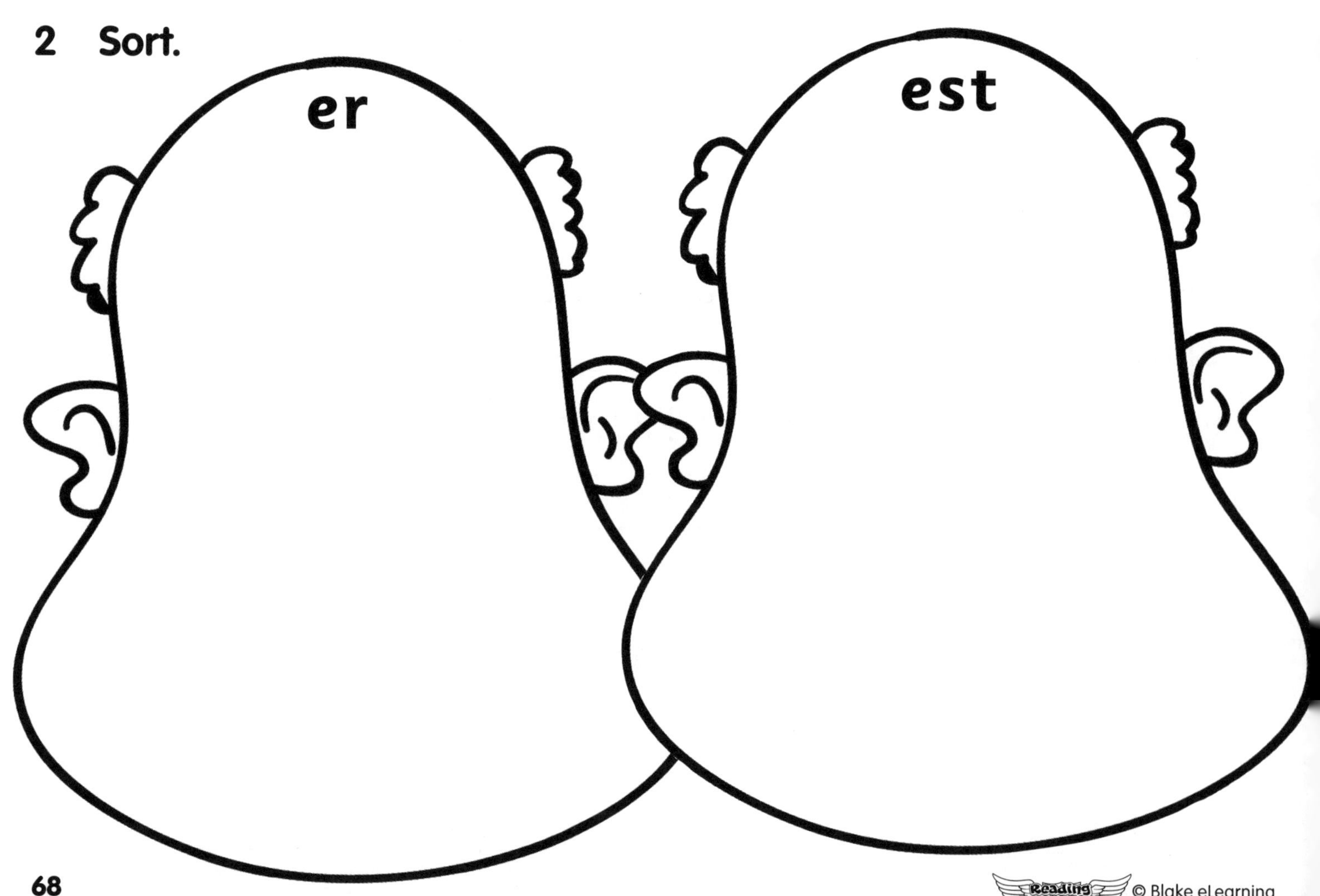

Suffixes – er, est

3 Complete each sentence with a list word.

An elephant is ______________ than a zebra.

That was the ______________ joke I have ever heard.

The blue whale is the ______________ animal in the world.

That was the ______________ assignment we've done this term.

I am neater and ______________ than my sister.

Challenge words

4 Copy each challenge word.

thinnest	______________	happiest	______________
scariest	______________	healthier	______________
fluffier	______________	healthiest	______________
curliest	______________	angrier	______________
happier	______________	angriest	______________

5 Complete the sentence with a challenge word.

That breed of chicken has ______________ feathers than that other breed.

She seems ______________ since she got a pet.

Her hair is the ______________ I have ever seen!

That movie was the ______________ I have ever seen!

6 Choose it. Circle and rewrite the correct word to complete the sentence.

Muesli was the [healthiest] [healthyest] option for breakfast. ______________

If you tease that dog it will just get [angrier] [angriest]. ______________

I snapped the [thinnest] [thinest] branch. ______________

Tricky words

1 Copy each list word.

I	______	with	______	pretty	______
again	______	there	______	who	______
always	______	off	______	mother	______
next	______	here	______	father	______
have	______	around	______	outside	______
were	______	wanted	______	when	______
things	______	school	______		

2 Meaning. Which list word means?

a place for teaching and learning ______

any space that is not inside ______

a female parent ______

a male parent ______

3 Opposites. Write the opposite.

on	______	unwanted	______
ugly	______	without	______
inside	______	never	______

4 Complete the sentence with a list word.

Our neighbours ______ a huge trampoline.

I took ______ my shoes before entering the house.

We spun ______ in circles.

We need to get off at the ______ bus stop.

Tricky words

5 Correct it. Write the word that is wrong correctly.

Ie am seven years old. __________

Mum told us to play outsde for a while. __________

I wantid to stay awake, but I fell asleep quickly. __________

I went to the zoo weth my grandma and grandpa. __________

I got it wrong, so had to start all over agein. __________

Challenge words

6 Copy each challenge word.

every __________	Christmas __________
once __________	people __________
happening __________	swimming __________
scared __________	women __________
favourite __________	February __________

7 Complete the sentence with a challenge word.

Mum and I went shopping for __________ presents.

On hot days we like to go __________ in the pool.

My birthday is in __________, the second month of the year.

Chocolate is my __________ flavour of ice-cream.

I am __________ of large dogs.

8 Silly sentences. Use as many challenge words as possible to make a silly story.

____

____

____

Suffixes – ment and ness

1 Copy each list word.

illness	__________	laziness	__________
payment	__________	fairness	__________
sadness	__________	enjoyment	__________
darkness	__________	thickness	__________
fitness	__________	blackness	__________
sickness	__________	pavement	__________
richness	__________	movement	__________
neatness	__________	statement	__________
weakness	__________	amazement	__________
softness	__________	treatment	__________

2 Missing letters. Write the missing letters to make a list word.

fit _ _ _ _	enjoy _ _ _ _	soft _ _ _ _
thick _ _ _ _	black _ _ _ _	dark _ _ _ _

3 Unscramble these list words.

ntmepay	__________	ntmeeattr	__________
nessfair	__________	momevent	__________
ntmepaev	__________	menteamaz	__________

4 Correct it. Write the word that is wrong correctly.

I felt sadnes when my friend moved away. __________

The darknes of night came quickly. __________

The concrete pavment was very hot. __________

The thikness of her hair made it hard to brush. __________

Suffixes – ment and ness

Challenge words

4 Copy each challenge word.

argument ______________ punishment ______________
excitement ______________ astonishment ______________
gentleness ______________ equipment ______________
willingness ______________ tiredness ______________
entertainment ______________ enchantment ______________

5 Complete the sentence with a challenge word.

My brother and I always have an ______________ about who sits in the front seat.

Dad made us help him as ______________ for our bad behaviour.

When camping, you must remember to bring the right ______________.

The wizard put an ______________ on the castle.

Thinking about the holidays filled me with ______________.

7 Choose it. Circle and rewrite the correct challenge word to complete the sentence.

It was her [willingness] [wilngess] to learn that made her a good student. ______________

We stared in [astonesment] [astonishment] at our teacher's new haircut. ______________

They hired a clown as [entertainment] [enterteinmnt] for the party. ______________

RULES AND GENERALISATIONS

Plurals

s, es
The prefixes *s* and *es* show plural nouns.
hat → *hats* glass → *glasses*

s, ves
For some nouns that end in *f* or *fe* change the *f* or *fe* to *v* then add *es*, leaf → *leaves*.
Some nouns that end in *f* or *fe* just need *s*, cliff → *cliffs*.

y
For some nouns and verbs that end in *y*, change it to *i* before adding *es*.
baby → *babies* city → *cities* try → *tries*

Prefixes

A prefix is added to the beginning of a word to make a new word with a slightly different meaning.

un
The prefix *un* turns the word into its opposite.
lock → *unlock* do → *undo* fair → *unfair*

Suffixes

A suffix is added to the end of a word to make a new word with a slightly different meaning.

ed
For past tense verbs simply add *ed*, mix → *mixed.*
When the verb ends in *e*, just add *d*, smile → *smiled.*
If a verb ends in *short vowel* + *consonant*, double the consonant then add *ed*, grip → *gripped.*

ing
For many verbs just add *ing*, walk → *walking.*
If the verb ends in *e*, drop the *e* before adding *ing*, care → *caring.*
If a verb ends in *short vowel* + *consonant*, double the consonant then add *ing*, clap → *clapping.*

ly
Adding the *ly* turns an adjective into an adverb, slow → *slowly.*
If the adjective ends in *y*, change the *y* to *i* before adding *ly*, easy → *easily.*

ful, less
Turn a noun or verb into an adjective by adding *ful* or *less*. pain → *painful* use → *useless*

er, est
To compare two nouns, add *er* to an adjective, short → *shorter.*
To compare MORE than two nouns, add *est* to an adjective, tall → *tallest.*
If the adjective ends in *e*, just add *r* or *st*, nice → nicer or *nicest.*
If the adjective ends in *y*, change the *y* to *i* then add *er* or *est*, happy → happier or *happiest.*

ment
Adding *ment* to a verb turns it into a noun.
enjoy → *enjoyment* pay → *payment* amaze → *amazement*

ness
Adding *ness* to an adjective turns it into a noun, weak → *weakness.*
If the adjective ends in *y*, change it to *i* before adding *ness*, tidy → *tidiness.*